T0134095

Data Science Without Makeup

Data Science Without Makeup

A Guidebook for End-Users, Analysts, and Managers

Mikhail Zhilkin

CRC Press
Taylor & Francis Group
Boca Raton London New York

CRC Press is an imprint of the
Taylor & Francis Group, an **informa** business

First edition published 2022
by CRC Press
6000 Broken Sound Parkway NW, Suite 300, Boca Raton, FL 33487-2742

and by CRC Press
2 Park Square, Milton Park, Abingdon, Oxon, OX14 4RN

CRC Press is an imprint of Taylor & Francis Group, LLC

Library of Congress Cataloging-in-Publication Data
Names: Zhilkin, Mikhail, author.
Title: Data science without makeup : a guidebook for end-users, analysts and managers / Mikhail Zhilkin.
Description: First edition. | Boca Raton : CRC Press, 2022. | Includes bibliographical references and index.
Identifiers: LCCN 2021020489 | ISBN 9780367523220 (hbk) | ISBN 9780367520687 (pbk) | ISBN 9781003057420 (ebk)
Subjects: LCSH: Databases. | Quantitative research. | Computer science.
Classification: LCC QA76.9.D32 Z44 2022 | DDC 005.74—dc23
LC record available at https://lccn.loc.gov/2021020489

ISBN: 978-0-367-52322-0 (hbk)
ISBN: 978-0-367-52068-7 (pbk)
ISBN: 978-1-003-05742-0 (ebk)

DOI: 10.1201/9781003057420

Typeset in Bookman
by codeMantra

contents

I
the ugly truth

II
a new hope

foreword

Walking into an interview in trainers, jogging bottoms, and a flowery T-Shirt and impressing the panel takes some doing yet Mikhail is a man who has accomplished this.

The interview was my first encounter with Mikhi, who throughout the interview highlighted potential pitfalls in what we asked, the importance of simplicity, and the need to get rough and ready results which can be utilized effectively. As part of the performance and medical team we knew we had a lot of data that needed exploring further and a lot of questions that needed answering. Games can be played every 3 days, so exploration of the data needs to be done quickly, efficiently, and thoroughly evaluated for any inaccurate information. Having come from a background of data science in the "real world," working in the gambling and gaming industry, this would be a new test for Mikhi. Data points are collated daily in vast amounts on highly valuable assets. We knew we needed someone who was able to understand the importance of moving quickly to assess any deviations while understanding that this would be a continuous working progress, building an infrastructure for accessible data around the football club. With Mikhi's dry humor and diverse thinking we have a valuable asset who can turn around untidy data sets quickly into "rough and ready" informed practice, while highlighting any potential inefficiencies within the data sets (from a man who has turned up to meetings with a T-Shirt saying "I may be wrong but it's highly unlikely"—it's likely the finger is being pointed at one of the other members of the performance and medical team!) and fixing them. Many car journey conversations and email threads have been exchanged on how we can use the data to "change the game" to provide informed insight into best practices. Breaking down the questions into the finer details so we can get the answer to the real question we are looking for. Once that is decided, the next step requires a lot of delving into dirty data.

Dirty data. The joys that every aspiring data scientist must be aware of. Unfortunately for the data scientist in football, the data itself has been pulled together by humans in Excel spreadsheets, written in word, and occasionally, scribbled on the back of yesterday's training report. Much of the initial time spent for Mikhi was tidying up erroneous data sets (sometimes managed by computer illiterate individuals!) with examples including spelling the same name 5 different ways, full stops hidden in Excel files, and poorly organized data sets. Many nights have been spent pulling data together to provide insight at short notice, with Mikhi steering the ship toward the correct insight, navigating through the choppy waters of misinterpretation (correlation does not necessarily mean causation) and bias (at the end of the day what human does not have beliefs in the background). The job of the data scientist is to stay neutral providing the real insight while highlighting the potential misconceptions the data (when understood incorrectly) can provide. Mikhi manages to provide us with a filter which tells us whether the data compliments or contradicts or does not really provide us a full insight on theories that keeps us on the right path toward "changing the game."

At the end of the day, from the understandings that data science has provided us within football, simplicity is key. You are there not only to analyze data, but also to spend time building databases, designing pretty visuals, with a lot of time spent tidying up data sets. The world of sport is beginning to see the importance of having people like Mikhi in place to manage the vast amounts of data. In a world where data is more voluminous and overpowering than before, it is important to have the people in place to bring it under control and disseminate it with the correct methods. As this book highlights, data science is growing in importance, but potential pitfalls remain. Mikhi is well versed to discuss and educate in this space, providing a humorous twist on some of the learnings he has had over his years of experience. He is pioneering in the world of data science in football, ensuring he is educating people in best practice for housing data (making his life easier), often reminding people to "think like a computer" when preparing data sets, reducing complexities, and focusing on what the required input is.

For a man who gave the first impression walking through our door that he was about to have a relaxing weekend on the sofa, he has been a key part of a team that has managed to embed a data infrastructure that interlinks departments throughout a world-renowned football club. His experiences to date illustrate that his opinion is one that should be valued. I am sure you, the reader, will gain some sort of enlightenment, a few good stories, and some humor, while getting a sneak peek behind the smoke and mirrors of the sexiest job in the 21st century....

Tom Allen
Lead Sports Scientist at Arsenal FC
June 2021

preface

The idea behind this book is to counterbalance the hype around data science.

The goal is not to deny how useful data science can be when done right, but to warn about how useless or even harmful when done wrong, and to show how difficult it is to stay on the right path.

This is not a textbook. It does not contain formulas, code snippets, or step-by-step instructions on how to "leverage data." Instead, it offers ideas that one is unlikely to hear at a data science conference, as well as many real-life examples that show data science in the cold light of day, warts and all.

There are quite a few books and countless articles and blog posts on how to start a career in data science, be a good data scientist or run a data science team. Many of them offer good advice. The idea behind this book is neither to argue with them nor to go along, but rather to complement the existing riches of material. If other books mostly spotlight the narrow path to success, this one draws attention to the countless possibilities to find oneself in a roadside ditch.

This book is aimed at a broad audience. It was mostly written from a data scientist's point of view, but you do not have to be a data scientist to get something out of it.

- If you are an aspiring data scientist, this book will help you to be enthusiastic about data science not because you are not aware of its problems and hardships, but in spite of knowing about them.

- If you are already a practicing data scientist, this book will offer you a new perspective, and possibly show you that you are not alone in your doubts and dark thoughts. It covers a wide range of data science activities, so if you are focused exclusively on machine learning or AI, this book may be too broad for you.

- If you are someone who manages a team of data scientists and/or is involved in hiring them, this book will deepen your understanding of what it is like to be a data scientist, what qualities you may want to look for and nurture, and how to separate the wheat from the chuff.

If you are none of the above but are simply curious about this data science thing everyone is talking about, this book will invite you behind the door with "The sexiest job of the 21st century" sign and show you what data science looks without makeup.

how to read this book

The basic principle you are probably familiar with: left to right, top to bottom.

There is an occasional pull quote to highlight an important idea. If you only read the pull quotes you will have a good grasp of what this book is about, though I do hope you will read the rest as well.

A section marked with a vertical line on the left contains a real-life story, usually from my personal experience, that illustrates a point.

At the end of each chapter, there is a little glossary explaining concepts and terms that may be less known, a list of cited books and articles, and chapter's endnotes with web links and whatever else did not quite fit in the main text.

author

Mikhail Zhilkin is a data scientist at Arsenal F.C. Before joining the London-based football club in 2018, he spent 4 years working on the *Candy Crush* franchise of mobile games.

Mikhail graduated from Moscow Institute of Physics and Technology with a master's degree in Applied Physics and Mathematics in 2006. He has worked in Russia, Japan, and Sweden. He now lives and works in the UK.

I

the ugly truth

There is a lot of hype around data science.

Not all enthusiasm around data science and machine learning (one of its subdomains) is misplaced. Personally, I am very excited about many things people have been doing with data: deep neural nets, language models, self-driving cars—the list gets longer every day. But it is important to tell the difference between legitimate advancements and hollow buzzwords.

Too often, when people are talking about data science—whether in front of a large crowd at a conference or in a cozy meeting at the office—they use phrases like "data-driven" or "artificial intelligence" as a way to switch on a big "APPLAUSE" sign. If you ask them what exactly they mean, or how they suggest it be implemented, you are unlikely to get a substantive answer. The speaker was not describing a potential state of reality, they just wanted the audience to clap.

"Data is the new oil," a phrase thrown around since 2006, has some truth to it. There are many useful applications for data mining and machine learning, and, generally speaking, the more data the better. But following this maxim blindly, one will end up with the business plan of underpants-stealing gnomes[1]:

Phase 1   → Phase 2 → Phase 3
Collect underpants   ?   Profit

Replace "underpants" with "data" and you will get many companies' approach to becoming data driven. "Let's collect the data and crunch it, and we'll change the game," they seem to be thinking.

And if there is anything better than data, then it is "big data." Having been in use since the 1990s, the term really took off in the 2010s. These days, it has been my experience that it is rarely used

DOI: 10.1201/9781003057420-1

by people who are working with massive amounts of structured and unstructured data that generally requires parallel computing. It has become one of the buzzwords that find their place in headlines and conference titles, regardless of their relevance.

Sticking with the metaphor, if data is oil, then to make use of it one needs to turn it into fuel and feed that fuel into the business-driving engine. Without these extra steps, you are just standing next to a barrel, looking silly. Which brings us to another overused phrase: "Data scientist is the sexiest job of the 21st century." Yes, the magical unicorn who will take your data and produce "insights" or some other "business value." I am a data scientist myself, and I have got a lot of time for my comrades. It is as good a job as any other. But most data scientists spend most of their time not being scientists, but rather plumbers and cleaners. Sometimes, monkeys.[2]

Reality never lives up to expectations based on a talk heard at a conference. People talk a lot about "digital transformation," "leveraging data," and "disrupting the industry." More often than not,

> Reality never lives up to expectations based on a talk heard at a conference.

there is little substance behind phrases like that. When a business is actually becoming data-driven, you are more likely to hear some of the following expressions:

- Data collection
- Event logging
- ETL (extract-transform-load—a widely used term, which basically means moving, processing, and storing data)
- Database, data lake, data warehouse
- A/B testing
- Model training, tuning, deployment into production

A data scientist, no matter how talented, is unlikely to be enough to transform your business. You would not be the first company to hire one, sit them down in front of a computer, and look at them expectantly, only to find out that you need to hire more people, with different skill sets, as well as invest heavily in data infrastructure and very slowly start changing company culture.

This is a long, hard road, along which you will learn that:

- You should have hired a data engineer who can do some data science, not a data scientist who can do some data engineering.

- There is a world of difference between a good data scientist and a bad one, but it is not always trivial to tell them apart in an interview.
- You cannot compensate poor quality of your data with advance machine learning algorithms. (You will get familiar with "RIRO"—rubbish in, rubbish out.)
- Things you thought hard can be done quickly, and things you thought trivial take time.
- Data science is done by people, people with cognitive biases and other limitations of the human brain.
- You can bring data-driven insights to people, but you cannot make people act on them.
- Most people do not want data, they want a confirmation of what they are already thinking.
- It is easy to lie with statistics (and there is a book[3] on how to do it).
- There is perceived value of data science, and there is actual value, and the two are often very different.
- Sometimes, when people say "A.I.," what they have actually got is a spreadsheet.

* * *

The first part of this book covers the following topics:

- What is data science? What do data scientists do? Where does data come from?
- What actually happens when someone is doing data science? What can possibly go wrong?
- Is human brain the perfect tool for dealing with data? If not, why?

Whether you are yourself a data scientist, or are working with data scientists, or want to become one, my hope is that the following chapters will help counterbalance the hype and unbridled optimism surrounding data science.

notes

1 *South Park* / season 2 / episode 17.

2 "Data monkey" is a derogatory term for a data analyst who spends most of their time pulling data and creating useless presentations to please senior management.

3 *How to Lie with Statistics* / Darrell Huff / 1982 W. W. Norton & Company.

what is data science

Once upon a time, I went to a data science conference. It was one of my first such events, and I was appropriately excited. I sat myself down in a big auditorium and prepared to be, if not blown away, then at the very least educated and entertained. Instead, I had to sit through a panel discussion that revolved around a single question— "What is a data scientist?"

It was not a question that had kept me awake at night. I already knew that what I did at work was called "data science." I just wanted to learn more about it and get better at it.

My hope is that you are, too, more interested in learning about data science in the real world, what actually goes on, and dos and don'ts rather than read through textbook definitions. This book *is* about this kind of stuff. Yet before we sink our teeth into it, let's briefly discuss:

- what data science is,
- what it is for,
- where data comes from, and
- why it is important to understand your data.

what data science is

Since you are reading this book, one could safely assume you have got at least a vague idea about what data science is. However, the range of things people can mean when the say "data science" is rather broad, so it is best to make sure we are on the same page.

The term "data science" is most often used to describe the discipline which extends the field of statistics to incorporate advances in

DOI: 10.1201/9781003057420-2

computing. A "data scientist" is someone who *applies* data science to solve a wide range of problems, and the "scientist" part can be misleading to those unfamiliar with the terminology.

The Care and Feeding of Data Scientists (D'Agostino and Malone 2019), an excellent book on managing data science teams, defines four data scientist archetypes:

1. **Operational**: applying data science to the everyday functioning of the business.
2. **Product-focused**: working closely with a product team, needs to be business savvy, like the operational data scientist.
3. **Engineering**: building and maintaining the systems that power the work of the product or operational data scientists.
4. **Research**: tasked with advancing the state of the art, often in a field like deep learning or computer vision or natural language processing, without any explicit expectation that their work will be immediately useful to the company.

The kind of data science examined in this book is primarily done by operational and product-focused data scientists. It generally implies a broad range of activities and requires a broad range of skills. You may be familiar with the following Venn diagram by Drew Conway[1]:

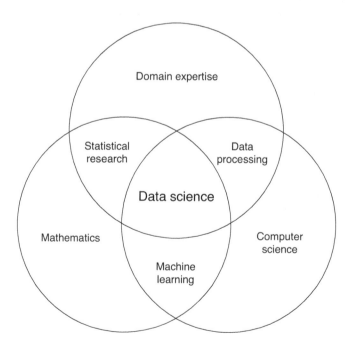

It should be noted that someone's proficiency in a domain is by no means a binary variable, 0 or 1, but rather a continuous one. Even then, it is a gross simplification. There is no one-dimensional scale in reality. For example, when it comes to mathematics, you may struggle to remember the formula for solving a quadratic equation, but as long as you are strong in the probability theory you are probably fine.

There is an important area missing on the diagram above—"Communication." We are going to talk more about communication skills in further chapters. For the moment, let's just add it to the diagram and have fun with the labels:

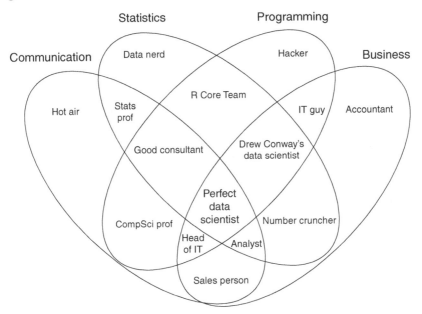

It would be hard to argue that one can be a good data scientist completely lacking skill in any of the four areas. But how good you need to be in each of them depends on the industry, organization, and what exactly you are asked to do.

In some organizations, data science efforts boil down to good old "business intelligence." It may be just a lonely business analyst (although they can still be called data scientist) answering ad-hoc questions ("How many of our users bet on golf?"). They can probably get away with the most rudimentary skills in each of the four areas.

More "data mature" organizations, especially those operating a website and/or mobile apps, invest in A/B testing—by no means a new method (clinical trials have been around for centuries). By randomly splitting users into groups and comparing their performance from a business point of view, these organizations can decide on the best course of action. By delving into exactly how one group out-performs others ("Is it the conversion rate? Transactions per day? Average transaction amount?"), the business can deepen their under-standing of user behavior. The data not only tells the business how things are, and how they can be depending on the business's choices, but also hints at why. This kind of data science typically puts higher requirements across the board:

- **Business**: design and analysis of an A/B test need to make sense from the business point of view. For example, if you run an A/B test on the existing users the results may be con-founded by users' reaction to change; it often makes sense to run a test on new users only, so that their experience is seamless.

- **Programming**: SQL queries become more complex. For exam-ple, if you had a very simple query to calculate percentage of paying users:

```
SELECT SUM(is_paying_user) / COUNT(*)
FROM users
```

you now need to calculate it separately for each A/B test group:

```
SELECT test_group, SUM(is_paying_user) / COUNT(*)
FROM users
JOIN abtest_groups USING(user_id)
GROUP BY test_group
```

- **Statistics**: reproducibility—Is the difference in test groups' behavior caused by the difference in user experience or is it a chance fluctuation?—becomes a concern.

- **Communication**: answers to questions like "Which test group performs better?" are generally more nuanced than to purely descriptive ones like "What is the average conversion rate?" And explaining p-values or Bayesian inference to a business-minded audience is a non-trivial communication challenge.

Organizations blessed with big enough samples can take finding patterns in data to next level by summoning the demons of "machine learning" and "predictive modelling." Generally, this is where marketing people start using the word "A.I." as if they were on commission. In this scenario, a data scientist's command of each of the four areas is likely to have to be stronger still.

* * *

On the personal level, while I have been called data scientist and not much else for about 8 years now, what I actually do has been changing quite a lot.

When I was just starting out, in early 2013, my usual workflow was:

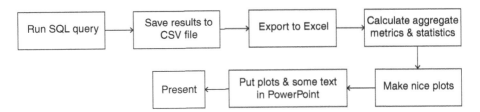

SQL, Excel, PowerPoint, and the ability to talk to people without drooling was all I needed.

A couple of online courses, a stack of books, and hundreds of hours on Stackoverflow (an online community, where people can ask and answer questions related to programming) later, my workflow now often is:

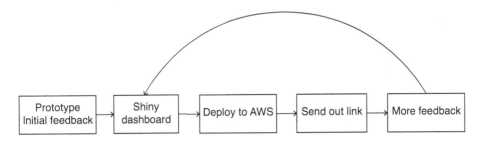

Or sometimes:

Some of the tools I am using these days were not yet available in 2013. An interactive online dashboard running on a virtual machine in the "cloud" would blow me-in-2013's mind. Yet, at the fundamental level, my job is still about taking raw data and transforming it into food for thought for other people.

Pivoting data in Excel and training a deep neural net may appear to belong to two different worlds, but most ideas discussed in this book are general enough to be applied to either of them or anything in between. I feel perfectly comfortable putting it all under the umbrella of data science.

what data science is for

Sometimes data science is the product, e.g., the model powering a recommendation engine. (I would offer an example, but there are quite a few recommendation engines, and it would be unfair to mention some of them and not the rest.)

Elsewhere, data science is an integral part of the product, e.g., the algorithm that estimates the delivery time in a food delivery app.[2]

In these scenarios, the impact of data science on the success of the product is obvious and directly measurable, for example, by means of A/B testing. However, in most companies, the causal chain from data science efforts to business goals—the "data impact pathway," if you will—is longer. Two examples adapted from my personal experience:

	Mobile Gaming Company	**Football Club**
Actual profit	In-app purchases	TV rights, tickets, merchandise, sponsors
Core product	Game	On-pitch performance
Direct influence	Game development team	Players
Principal decision-making	Producer	Head coach
Indirect influence	Business performance manager	Head of performance/ Fitness coach/Sports scientist
Hope to make a difference	Data scientist	

Let's consider a hypothetical scenario in the case of mobile gaming company:

A data scientist has produced a piece of analysis that shows that a particular game mechanic monetizes poorly. These results need to make their way—most likely in the form of a presentation—first to the respective business performance manager, and then to the game producer. (Why a business performance manager is needed is a separate story.) The producer may decide to do away with that game mechanic and replace those levels in the game that utilize it. The task is created for the development team, and in due time, the required changes are implemented and pushed to the production server.

If the above sounds too smooth, it is because it is the "ideal world" scenario. The data impact pathway is prone to breaking up at every step:

- The business performance manager may decide, justifiably or not, that the analysis is inconclusive, or otherwise unfit to be widely circulated.
- The producer may decide that the team need to prioritize developing new game mechanics over getting rid of existing ones.
- The game team may be fond of the game mechanic they worked so hard on and push back with all they have against the suggested changes.

This is exactly what I once observed when working on the widely popular *Candy Crush Saga*. A data scientist (not me) ran a comprehensive analysis of various "blockers" (things that make it harder for the player to clear a level), which showed that one particular blocker performed very poorly in terms of player engagement and monetization. A clear case was made for re-designing several game levels and replacing this blocker with one of the better performing ones.

There was an impressive pushback from the game team, with many people being very fond of the unfortunate blocker. The suggested changes were implemented eventually, but there was a real possibility that things would have remained the same. In that case, the data analysis would have proved useless.

* * *

I also witnessed a counterexample, a year or two later.

The company's culture was growing more data-driven. When the game team working on the sequel—*Candy Crush Soda Saga*—created a set of levels with a new game mechanic, they were *asking* to see how these levels performed compared to the baseline.

The results were discouraging. The players clearly did not enjoy the new game mechanic, with both engagement and monetization down. The game team, having asked the question themselves, heeded the data, abandoned the new game mechanic, and promptly replaced the experimental levels.

> Data science has a much better chance of making a difference when it responds to people's inquiry rather than barges in uninvited.

Data science has a much better chance of making a difference when it responds to people's inquiry rather than barges in uninvited.

A broken link in a data impact pathway simply renders the whole thing meaningless. One could possibly argue that even unsuccessful efforts may produce change in how people perceive data science (the often-mentioned "data-driven culture"), but the opposite is more likely: people see more value in data science when it results in visible changes, and less when it does not.

And when data science does lead to an actual change, it can only happen if it succeeds in changing opinions. Unless data science is the product or part of the product, it can only lead to changes in the product by changing someone's opin-

> Unless data science is the product, the end goal of data science is to change opinions.

ion first. This needs to be someone who can affect the product directly or indirectly and, depending on the data impact pathway, multiple opinions may need to be changed. But the fact remains: Unless data science is the product, the end goal of data science is to change opinions.

To be clear, it would be obviously wrong to start out with the intent of changing a particular opinion. It would be nothing but confirmation bias (which we will discuss in more detail later) in reverse. Sometimes data will confirm what people were already believing. However, if data never contradicts what people already believe, then what is the point?

Imagine that you are designing a free-to-play mobile game, and you run an A/B test whenever there is an important design decision.

- Should the earlier levels be easier or harder to maximize long-term retention and conversion?
- Should extra lives cost less or more to maximize the respective revenue?

- Should you release new levels every week or every other week to get higher return on the level designers' time?

If every A/B test only confirms your original guess, then either you have a perfect intuition (unlikely) or the process is broken (much more likely). Either way, the game looks exactly as it would have, had you not been using A/B testing at all. The impact of data is zero.

Now, if some of the A/B tests showed that your intuition was wrong, and you decided to go down the path you would not have originally chosen, the difference between how the game is performing and how it would have performed is the added value of your data efforts.

Ironically, the worse your intuition, the more you will benefit from being "data-driven." I could see that with injury prediction in football. While injury prediction is often the first thing that springs to everyone's mind at a mention of "football players' physical data," the reality is:

- The data available for each individual player in your team is limited, and for players of other teams even more so. The sample size is small, which is exacerbated by players frequently changing clubs.
- The intuition of people working directly with the players (S&C coaches, physiotherapists, etc.), based on years of experience, sets a high bar, which predictive data models are yet to beat, to my best knowledge.

This is why when someone tells me that "change" is the wrong word, and that data science should "inform" opinions, I respond that data science only adds value when the opinion of someone important has been changed. To "inform" can result in either "confirm" or "disprove," and it is the "disprove" part where data science adds value.

Throughout my career, I often heard people say "It would be interesting to see..."

This is especially often said by someone present at a meeting who has got neither a reason to be there nor anything substantial to contribute. Their curiosity does not come from a legitimate need to make a business decision. This is just a conscious or subconscious attempt to take part, to leave a mark, to show others that you are not a waste of space. This person is not going to put any effort into answering their own question. Even if they could. Usually they cannot.

Such questions can be safely ignored. You can even sincerely agree that yes, it would be interesting to see, wouldn't it, before moving on with your life. There will not be any follow-through, as there was no intention to actually answer the question.

* * *

Sometimes, people may be coming from a sincere belief that answering a question will be beneficial, and then your job is to help them figure out whether or not that is the case.

Once I was asked to investigate if there was correlation between self-reported and objective sleep quality data, objective data coming from a sleep-tracking device that we were considering. The following dialogue ensued:

Me: What happens if we see strong correlation?
Them: Then we will be using the sleep-tracking device.
Me: What happens if we *do not* see strong correlation?
Them: Um... I guess we will be using the device anyway, as we have got more faith in its measurements than in self-reported quality of sleep.
Me: So, whatever the outcome of the analysis, we will be using the device?
Them: Um... Yes...
Me: If we are going to do the same thing anyway, would it make sense to prioritize analyzing something else, something that can potentially change what we do?
Them: Yeah, probably...

why it is important to understand your data

"An analyst is not as good as the tools he can use, but as good as his understanding of the data"—I was told this before I even got familiar with the term "data analysis," by my first manager

> An analyst is only as good as their understanding of the data.

when I moved to Sweden in 2012. I do not remember much from that time, but these words will always ring true.

An analyst is only as good as their understanding of the data.

Learning the ins and outs of a data set at your disposal is not something every analyst wakes up for. I am definitely guilty of starting many a data analysis with nothing but a naïve hope that I will learn enough about the data I am using as I go. I am sure it varies from person to person, but unless you are of a very patient and methodical temperament, it can be very tempting to dive into the project headfirst. After all, the desire to find insights into data is what got you into this line of business in the first place.

This is another example of the Goldilocks principle (just the right amount). You definitely do not want to know too little, but you do not want to become obsessed with every tiny detail either.

Knowing too little about your data is problematic in an obvious way.

Before I joined King as data scientist, I worked at a fintech company called Klarna. A business analyst was giving a presentation on profits and margins. One of the figures he was showing was suspiciously high. So high that someone, for once, did have a question. The analyst might have lacked in competence, but not in confidence, and responded along the lines of "the data says so." Unfortunately for him, a more knowledgeable person pointed out that the column "amount" in the database the analyst used in his calculations was in cents, not in dollars. Curtains down.

At the other extreme lies wanting to know everything about your data. This is often impractical and potentially detrimental to the task at hand.

Especially when dealing with "wide" data, there may be so many columns (several hundreds is not unheard of) that finding out what exactly each of them contains just does not make sense. As long as you have verified your assumptions about the data set as a whole, and the handful of columns you are going to use, your understanding of the data is in all likelihood adequate in the context of your project.

* * *

To understand your data, you generally need to learn where it comes from, how it was collected, and why it was collected in the first place.

When data is collected manually, you also need to consider the human factor. Manual data collection may result in two types of errors:

- **Accidental**: It is not a question if people will make mistakes. The question is what you can do about it. At the very least, you can identify and flag values that fall outside the reasonable range.

  For example, if someone writes down an athlete's body weight, a trivial check of whether it is a number between 50 and 100 kg (sensible for a soccer player) is likely to catch the majority of typos. A more sophisticated sanity check would be to compare the new entry against the last one for the same athlete and flag the former if the difference exceeds 1–2 kg (again, sensible for people trying to maintain their body weight).

- **Data tampering**: Unfortunately, sometimes people may try to bend the truth itself.

Kate Laskowski shares a detailed and educational story[3] about several retractions caused by people tampering with data:

"Science is built on trust. Trust that your experiments will work. Trust in your collaborators to pull their weight. But most importantly, trust that the data we so painstakingly collect are accurate and as representative of the real world as they can be.

And so when I realized that I could no longer trust the data that I had reported in some of my papers, I did what I think is the only correct course of action. I retracted them."

There were a lot of duplicate entries in the data set, something that was not easy to discover without digging into the data. With duplicate entries removed, the research results no longer held.

where data comes from

If you are an aspiring data scientist going through online courses, "bootcamps," perhaps even reading books, then you are probably used to data being provided when you are given a task. A data set is just there, and all you need to do is start doing things to it: filter, aggregate, visualize, fit a model—all the sexy things one is supposed to do to a data set. The more practical and/or advanced courses may even suggest that you have got to "clean" your data: validate columns, identify obvious errors, handle missing values... These being valuable and necessary skills notwithstanding, at no point are you asked to question where the data came from in the first place, how it was collected, and—often an important question—why.

If you are a senior executive, you have probably done your share of talking about the importance of data, how your organization "leverages" its data, and how "data-driven" your business is or should be. You might have even been overheard saying "Data is the new oil." Yet you do not concern yourself with what exactly is your data. It is just something you are collecting from your users, right? How complicated can it be?

It is the people in between the above two cases, people "in the field" actually collecting data one way or another, and those tasked with making sense of it that have first-hand knowledge of numerous problems related to data collection.

When I was working with *Candy Crush data*, the most important game events we collected were "game start" and "game end," which were triggered when the player started playing a level and either completed it or failed.

Most of the time things were as you would expect: one game start followed by one game end. Nice and clean.

Sometimes, there would be a game start but no game end. Not much of a mystery: the player probably "force-quit" the game, so the app had no opportunity to generate a game end event.

Less often still, one would see a game end without a corresponding game start. This made no sense: one physically cannot finish a level without starting it. Assuming the game start event was generated, the only possible explanation was that it simply never made it to the database. With billions of events being processed daily, it should not come as a surprise that a handful simply get lost.

> One feature of "big data" is that it is likely to contain various imperfections, and a data scientist working with it must not assume the ideal-world scenario.

One feature of "big data" is that it is likely to contain various imperfections, and a data scientist working with it must not assume the ideal-world scenario.

The biggest risk of things falling through the cracks is when there is a disconnect between people responsible for data collection and processing, and people responsible for data analysis. And since lines between departments and teams are usually drawn based on what people do, these two groups are likely to be separated both organizationally and physically.

We easily underestimate how much of a difference it makes if people sit in the same room or not. If I have got a question for another person, and I can ask them just by vocalizing it, perhaps even without turning my head, the risk of a communication breakdown is small. But if I have to go to a different floor that person might as well be located in an overseas office—I am either sending them an email or deciding that it is not that important and better just leave it. (Tools like Slack or HipChat may mitigate the situation somewhat, but it is a far cry from being on the same team and sitting in the same room.) This personal experience is confirmed by research (Waber et al. 2014) that shows the farther apart the people are, the less they communicate.

I spent a year at a sports betting company, which handled thousands of sporting events and millions of bet offers.

There was often a situation when a bet offer (e.g., Liverpool to finish in the top four in the Premier League) was technically valid, i.e., the season was not over yet, but no bookmaker was actually taking any more bets on it, because it was a mathematical certainty, or so close to it that it did not make sense to keep the bet offer open.

The back-end developers in charge of the platform had decided, at some point in the distant past, that in such situation the odds were to be set at exactly 1 (or 0:1 in fractional notation), and not shown to users. It was a neat solution that did not require any significant changes in the software architecture.

A few years down the road, when the company embarked on the path of becoming data-driven and hired a few analysts, they would often have to calculate average odds of this or that as part of their research efforts. These analysts had not been part of the historical design decision and did not know they had to filter out any bet offer with odds = 1, which caused quite a bit of unnecessary pain.

You can easily picture different problems that may be caused by such a disconnect between, in this case, developers and analysts, but it is not so easy to decide who was at fault (if anyone at all) and what practical solution would have prevented that from happening. Should the developers have provided extensive documentation on every little quirk in the system? Well, they could not possibly foresee all the ways the data was going to be used. Should the analysts carefully have verified their assumptions about the data? Well, it is always a good idea to verify one's assumptions, but if an analyst is to question every aspect of a data collection system they will essentially have to know everything the system's developers know.

And even when developers and analysts work as a team, there is no guarantee of a smooth sailing.

When I worked as a data scientist on *Candy Crush Jelly Saga* (the third game in the *Candy Crush* franchise), we decided to implement some additional event tracking to get more insights into player behavior. The idea was clear and thought out, I could walk over to the developer who would write the actual tracking code, he was as helpful as they come and would even show me around the game code...

If this were a TV show, the screen would now read: *Five iterations later...*

Yes, this little piece of data-generating code took us five or six iterations to get right. One or two of them were to fix implementation bugs, but the rest were due to lack of foresight. When you design something "on paper," things often look deceptively straightforward. Only when the code is live and you look at the data it generates, do you realize that it is not exactly what you need, or that you cannot always tell one scenario from another, or that it would be much more useful if it also included this information...

I remember a time when I would often get frustrated talking to developers. I felt they made even the simplest thing sound complicated and every little task—a massive project. But with every experience of having to walk the entire path from design to implementation to real-life usage, which had been invariably humbling, I would be getting close to the realization that almost nothing is simple in the world of computers, software, and data.

> The world can be perceived as simple only when we are thinking at a high level of abstraction.

The world can be perceived as simple only when we are thinking at a high level of abstraction.

For example, if you are building a predictive model for football matches, you will probably want to have a variable that indicates which team play at home. Very simple. There is always the home team and the away team. Very simple. Until you come across a match played on a "neutral" stadium. It can be the final of a tournament, or a pre-season friendly played abroad, or perhaps the home team's stadium was unavailable. Or what if the game was

> Things get complicated even before you start analyzing data.

played at the home team's stadium, but no fans were allowed, which sometimes happens as a punishment? (And let's not even get started on the whole COVID-19 situation.) Very quickly the initially clear-cut picture becomes uncomfortably nuanced.

Things get complicated even before you start analyzing data.

* * *

Even when you understand exactly where your data comes from, who, why, and how collected it are equally important considerations.

Sometimes it is all very straightforward. Game start and game end events in *Candy Crush* are "fired" by specific segments in the programming code, without complicated rules or exceptions, and no-one has any interest in tampering with this data.

Sometimes there is only a thing or two to keep in mind. Using sports betting as an example, the database might have appeared to contain all bets placed by customers, but it actually had no record of bets there were not accepted due to insufficient funds in the customer's account or other such reasons. While this blind spot did not matter when calculating turnover and profit margin, it could make a difference in user experience and user behavior research.

And sometimes the way data is collected is absolutely crucial to its interpretation.

The coronavirus pandemic of 2020 was characterized by an unusually high public interest in all kinds of numbers and plots: number of infections, recoveries, severe cases... The whole world was following daily reports, full of various metrics, split by country or age group.

One of the key metrics was the number of confirmed cases. What many publications would fail to clarify was that to confirm a case, i.e., that a person had the virus, you needed to test them. And tests, especially in the early days, could be costly and time-consuming, which meant that they were used sparingly. Furthermore, availability of testing varied a lot from country to country.

The spectrum of testing coverage spans from testing no-one, which would result in zero confirmed cases (provided you ignored covid-19 symptoms or waved them off as "just a flu"), or testing the entire population, which would give you a complete picture, but is practically impossible.

Different countries could fall quite far from each other on this spectrum. On the one hand, you had South Korea, which had been able to ramp up testing quickly and tested many people across all age groups. On the other hand, you had Italy, which struggled with a massive outbreak in Lombardy and had to focus its efforts on testing older people and other high-risk groups.

Without considering the differences in testing between South Korea and Italy, one could conclude that the mortality rate was an order of magnitude higher in Italy.

* * *

Rob Kitchin, a social scientist in Ireland and the author of *The Data Revolution* (2014), has argued that instead of the word "data" (derived from Latin meaning "given") it would be more appropriate to think of it as "capta" (Latin for "taken"). Indeed, data is never given and is always the result of someone's observation and measurement.

In the world of data analytics, people often use the term "raw data," which can create an illusion of that data being the "ground truth," an objective and untouched representation of reality. This is misleading. The very process of collecting data inevitably requires some kind of "cooking."

Bowker (2008), an informatics professor, said it well: "Raw data is both an oxymoron and a bad idea; to the contrary, data should be cooked with care." There is no such thing as "raw" data.

> There is no such thing as "raw" data.

glossary

Business performance manager (BPM) is a role that does not necessarily exist or have the same name in all big data-driven companies. In this book, it is used for someone responsible for communicating data-driven insights into the product team and/or the rest of organization.

Wide data presents each variable in a separate column—unlike "narrow" or "long" data which has only two columns: variable name and variable value.

works cited

Memory Practices in the Sciences / Geoffrey C. Bowker / 2008 The MIT Press.

The Care and Feeding of Data Scientists / Michelangelo D'Agostino, and Katie Malone / 2019 O'Reilly Media.

The Data Revolution: Big Data, Open Data, Data Infrastructures and Their Consequences / Rob Kitchin / 2014 SAGE Publications.

"Workspaces That Move People" / Ben Waber, Jennifer Magnolfi, and Greg Lindsay / *Harvard Business Review* (2014).

notes

1 http://drewconway.com/zia/2013/3/26/the-data-science-venn-diagram.

2 https://www.businessinsider.com/deliveroo-uses-frank-algorithm-to-cut-delivery-times-by-20-2017-7.

3 https://laskowskilab.faculty.ucdavis.edu/2020/01/29/retractions/.

data science is hard

My first ever talk at a data analytics conference was titled "Why You Mustn't Listen to a Data Scientist" (Gaming Analytics Summit, March 3–4, 2016, London). A few years on, it is still the most passionate talk I have ever given. "Why?," I hear you ask.

At the time of the talk, I had only been a data scientist for 3 years, and I had only worked at King, which had by far the most data-driven culture of all places I have been at. Yet, in spite of the culture and all the brilliant people who worked there, I was growing more skeptical about the whole "data science" thing by the day. My skepticism was in stark contrast with the ever-present hype around data science. The hype permeated the media, the industry, and every conference I would attend.

It is only natural that practitioners praise their field. I have never met a marketeer who would openly say that marketing is overrated, or a game developer who would insist that playing games is a waste of time, or a personal trainer who would admit that they do not really know what they are doing. It is a self-preservation instinct to find meaning in what you do.

It is not that I ever doubt the potential of using data to improve the world. I am rather enthusiastic about what can be done in this area. It is why and how it is usually done that bothers me. Knowing what exactly goes into a sausage makes it so much harder to believe it is good for whoever eats it.

In most fields, outsiders tend to overestimate the value of ideas and underestimate the challenge of implementation. Data science is no exception. I find it disturbing that few people openly talk about how difficult it is to do data science the right way, and not turn it into a massive waste of resources. It is good to see that conversations have started around the ethical implications of machine learning and

DOI: 10.1201/9781003057420-3

around AI safety. These are important topics. Lofty topics. But we are still not talking about what is going on down below, in the trenches of day-to-day business intelligence and data analytics, at the level of spreadsheets and hastily cobbled together scripts. It is not an existential threat to the humankind, but it does deserve an occasional blog post, a talk at a conference, or perhaps even a book.

* * *

Since the job title "Data Scientist" was first printed on my business cards in 2013, the field of data science has been evolving nonstop. New best practices and tools have been popping up faster than one can read about them, let alone actually try them in battle conditions. Nonetheless, many of the problems are still here.

We are going to talk about the challenges of recruiting and managing data scientists in Part III of this book. This chapter is about the fundamental challenges faced by the individual data scientist working on their individual project.

A business analyst crunching numbers in a messy spreadsheet faces a different set of problems than a machine learning expert. Yet there are three primal difficulties that are known to anyone who has to extract value from data. I have given them poetic names:

- Iceberg of details
- Domino of mistakes
- No second chance

Let's go through these one by one.

iceberg of details

I am a data scientist working with the Medical and Performance team at the Arsenal football club. I am sitting in a cluttered office I share with a few people, enjoying my morning coffee amidst various sports-related bits of hardware. Our sports scientist (let's call him "Tom," because that is his name) walks in and says:

—Can we compare our physical outputs this season against the last?
Even if you are not familiar with the sport, the question may seem straightforward. The physical outputs can refer to the total distance players run in the course of a football match, or the distance covered

above a certain speed threshold, or even the distance covered while accelerating or decelerating—it is safe to assume Tom and I both know what we are talking about.

Also, let's not question the motivation behind the question. It is a good habit to always try and find out why people are asking a question, but for the purpose of this example let's assume that Tom's reasons are sound, and we are all on the same page.

So, this is the request I receive: "Compare our physical outputs this season against the last." You may notice that we are not suffering a great deal of detail yet. In this form, the request makes for a neat to-do item or presentation title. But. This is only the tip of the iceberg.

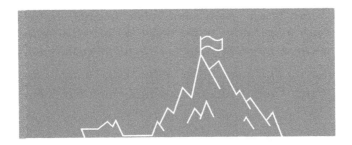

If this were my first project I might get to work straight away. But this is not my first project, and I come back at Tom with a whole bunch of questions that I know I will have to answer:

- Should we use data from all games, or should we discard FA Cup, League Cup, and Europa League games? (These are often played against much weaker opposition, which affects players' physical outputs.)

- We are one-third into the season and have only played a dozen games, an unusual proportion of which were away games against teams from the top half of the league table. (This often results in spending a lot of time defending and not doing much high-speed running.) Would it be accurate to compare the outputs this season so far against the entirety of the last season?

- Should we look at the average outputs of the entire team or individual players? (Some players have left since last season, some have arrived.)

- What should we do about players who only played a partial game (players who were substituted or came on as substitutes; or, more rarely, were sent off)? We could calculate outputs per minute, but what about players coming on only for the last few minutes of the game? Their per-minute values are likely to be skewed.

- How should we treat players who have played in different positions? For example, the outputs of someone like Pierre-Emerick Aubameyang will be quite different depending on whether he plays as center forward or wide midfielder. Same can be said for Granit Xhaka, who a few times had to leave his normal position of defensive midfielder and play as a full-back.

A quick glance below the waterline, and we are beginning to realize the actual size of the iceberg. The original request now comes with quite a footnote: "Premier League only. Same subset of games from last season. Individual outfield players. Only when they played in their 'primary' position. Appearances of 30 minutes or longer. Per-minute values."

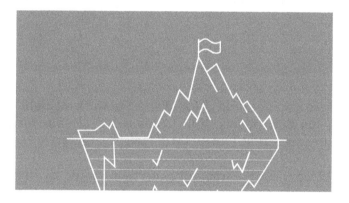

The request has become somewhat long-winded, and sports scientist Tom is having second thoughts about me being a valuable addition to the staff. Fortunately, I am done with Tom by this point. Less fortunately, the actual data analysis is only about to begin.

I have to carry on with my descent underwater, with the iceberg growing ever bigger. Even with the research question clarified, dealing with the actual, more often than not messy, data brings new challenges:

- I have to decide what data set I am going to use. There may be more than one data source available, and they will not necessarily lead to the same results. For example, physical data may be gathered by means of cameras that track players' position on the pitch or GPS units players wear underneath their shirts.

- I have to identify the variables (e.g., columns in database), and understand what values they contain and how they correspond to reality. For example, a column named "Player Position" is intuitive enough, but the fact that goalkeepers were encoded as "Goalkeeper" in one season and "GK" in the other has to be discovered and taken into account, lest I fail to exclude them from calculations consistently and end up comparing outfield players in one season to *all* players in the other.

- I have to carefully explore the data and "clean" it—something, you might have heard, that takes up to 80% or 90% of data scientists' time. Continuing the example of "Player Position" column, what positions can an outfield player occupy? Do I treat "DM" (defensive midfield) and "CM" (center midfield) as different positions? What about "LB" and "RB" (left- and right-back)—surely, they are essentially the same position from the fitness point of view? Wait... there are a lot of missing values in this column... a-ha, players who come on as substitutes do not get assigned a position value. Can I assume they played in their primary position, the one in which they have made most of their appearances?

This list can go on for a while. The simplicity of the original request is all but a distant memory. And I have not even begun writing the actual code for data extraction, transformation, and, possibly, visualization.

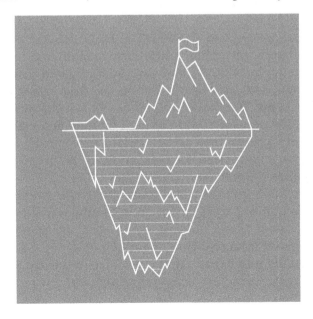

Eventually, I will have mapped out the iceberg in all its magnificence. If I do my job well, Tom will get a meaningful and succinct answer to his question. For example, "The average distance per minute is roughly the same as last season, but high-speed running has increased by about 2%." He will take it up to other people. People, who shall remain blissfully ignorant of all the nitty-gritty detail of how this insight has been arrived at.

* * *

This is not to say that the iceberg of detail is something exclusive to data science. In any industry, there is much more going on than what meets the eye of a casual observer. Still, I would argue that the chasm between how data science is perceived and how it is actually practiced is particularly wide. People do not wonder what is so difficult about building a house ("It is just walls and roof") or launching a space rocket ("You just ignite fuel and point the rocket where you want it to go"), but unless they have been in data science trenches, they tend to severely underestimate how many little details need to be taken care of.

domino of mistakes

Any data analysis beyond COUNT(*) is bound to be a complex and sequential process, involving multiple steps of diverse nature.

For a very simple example, let's say you have been tasked with calculating the average user spend within the first 7 days of installing a smartphone app. The marketing team will rely on your analysis in determining how much should be spent on user acquisition.

The company prides itself on being data-driven (who doesn't?) and everything you might need for this analysis is already stored in a sensibly organized database.

"Piece of cake," you think to yourself. "I will finish this before lunch and go home early, to work on my sumo wrestling prediction model."

"Yeah, right," thinks reality.

And as you dig into it, each and every step of the analysis presents a wonderful opportunity for screwing things up:

What you need to do	**How you screwed it up**
1 Find database table with users' payments	You use an outdated table: *financial_transactions* instead of *financial_transactions_v2*
	There is still data coming into the first table, generated by customers using old versions of the app, so you do not notice anything wrong, but you end up looking at early adopters who have not updated the app in a while instead of the current user base.
2 Find column that contains transaction amount in $	You see a column named *amount* and assume that's what you need, looking no further.
	Little do you know that the column contains transaction amount in local currency. The column you should have used is called *amount_usd*.
3 Find database table with users	You decide to use *installs* table, which has *install_id* column.
	You do not realize that one user may install the app on multiple devices. You should have used *users* table and *user_id* column.
	You are now calculating average spend per device rather than user, which makes a big difference, given that high spenders tend to use the app on more than one device.
4 Join users and payments	You use (INNER) JOIN on *installs* and *financial_transactions* instead of LEFT (OUTER) JOIN, thus filtering out users who have never paid.
	Instead of average spend per user, you are now calculating average spend per *paying* user. Big difference.
5 Calculate and report average spend	Without talking to anyone, you decide that calculating mean is not fancy enough, and that using median is better, as the result will not be skewed by "whales."
	Unfortunately, the marketing team needed precisely the mean, and were not aware that median is something else. After all, it was your job to "do the math."

You might look at the above examples and think that you would never do something so silly. If so, you either deserve a shrine dedicated to your infallibility, or you have been making silly mistakes but are yet to catch yourself.

I regularly embarrass myself making silly mistakes, but I have learnt to get over it. What keeps me awake at night is the thought about all mistakes I am not embarrassed about, because I have not noticed them.

Regardless of how prone to making mistakes you are, should you get things wrong at any one step of the process, you have potentially rendered the whole analysis essentially useless. Hence the analogy with a row of upright dominoes—if anyone gets knocked over then all the dominoes standing after it will fall, too. The error propagates all the way to the final result.

Even if the risk of making a critical mistake at each step is seemingly small, the total risk of a screw-up, which grows rapidly with the number of steps, quickly reaches unnerving levels. For example, if the probability of making a mistake at any one step of a data analysis task is 5% (optimistic much?) and independent from previous steps, this is what happens to the probability of arriving at the correct result as the number of steps goes up:

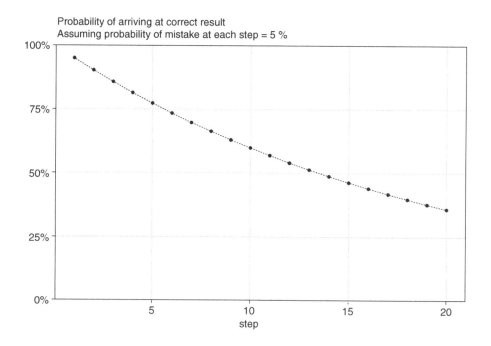

Another contributing factor is that data sciencing usually involves using a wide variety of tools.

Hadoop communication skills
Java
statistics
SQL R predictive
machine learning
Python SAS
computer science
data visualization

The set of tools a data scientist uses tends to change, sometimes every few months, at the very least every couple of years. SQL, NoSQL, KindaSQL, Big Data, Even Bigger Data, machine learning, data visualization frameworks, cloud computing... Both a blessing and a curse, this dooms a data scientist to what I call a "permanent state of noobery."

You may become well-versed in a certain domain, in using *some* of the tools, but there will always be less familiar areas and tools you are still getting the hang of. No surprise that many data scientists struggle to shake off the imposter syndrome (feeling that they are underqualified, and that their having the job they have is a mistake of the hiring process.)

The less experience you have got using a technology or a tool, the higher the risk of your using it incorrectly. Duh.

Saying "We all make mistakes" may soothe one's ego, but it will not make the analysis any less wrong.

> Saying "We all make mistakes" may soothe one's ego, but it will not make the analysis any less wrong.

no second chance

Unless you are working in a business where data is the product, data analytics plays a supporting role. Let's consider, for example, some kind of a software product, where the main feedback loop works roughly like this:

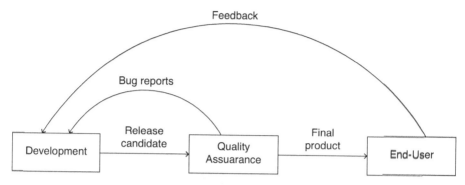

To make the product development fashionably data-**driven**, the company sets up a business intelligence team:

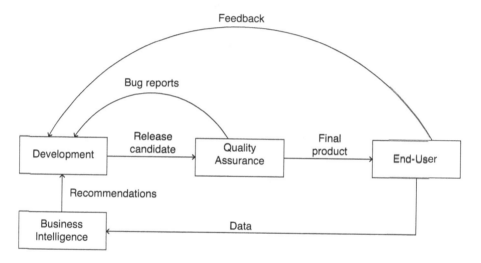

(The "data" arrow is never that simple in real life, and often introduces a host of new problems: data collection, data warehousing, data modeling, documentation, etc.)

If a developer makes a mistake and introduces a bug, and even if it gets through the Quality Assurance (QA) system undetected, as long as it affects the end-user in an obvious way it is likely to be reported, thus giving the developer a chance to make amends.

In contrast, if a business intelligence (BI) person makes a mistake in their analysis and delivers the wrong recommendation, it is very unlikely to come

> In data analysis, you rarely get a second chance.

back to them. In data analysis, you rarely get a second chance.

Furthermore, if a software end-user comes across a problem, there may be a workaround (e.g., the classic "turn it off and on again"). I cannot remember a single case when someone could "work around" an incorrect number or a misleading plot.

* * *

For a very simple example, let's consider the case of a mobile game, whose developers are tracking the average number of games per user, measured daily. We will generate some randomish data with a realistic weekly cycle (players are more active at weekend) and a gentle upward trend:

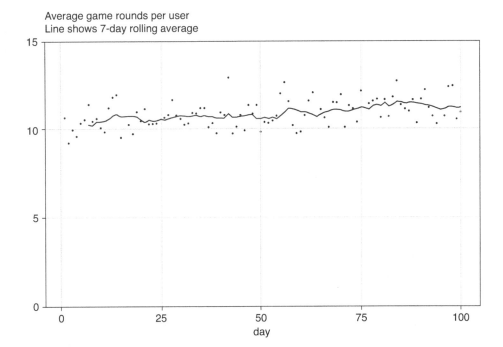

Now, let's imagine an A/B test was run for 50 days to compare this metric for two different implementations, with 50% of users in each test group:

Average game rounds per user
Line shows 7-day rolling average for each test group

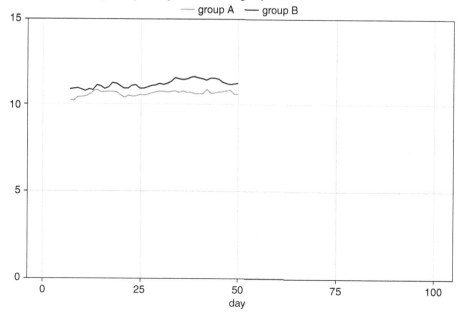

Implementation B is a clear winner. It outperforms implementation A by 5.3% on average, which is a massive uplift.

From day 51 onwards, all players are on implementation B:

Average game rounds per user
Line shows 7-day rolling average

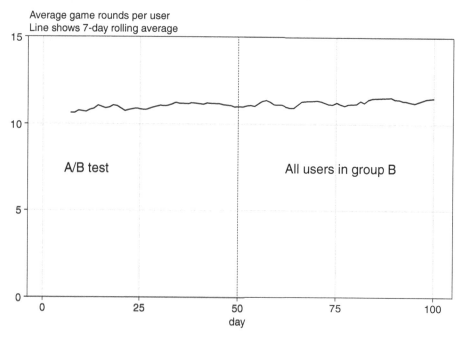

Success! Well done, everyone!

Except... The data analyst had mislabeled the columns in his spreadsheet, and it had actually been group A that had outperformed in the test. And even though the mistake is costly, no-one would immediately suspect that something was wrong just by looking at daily stats.

* * *

You might think that, even if there is no direct feedback from the end-user, the data analyst can simply use a QA process similar to that of the product development cycle:

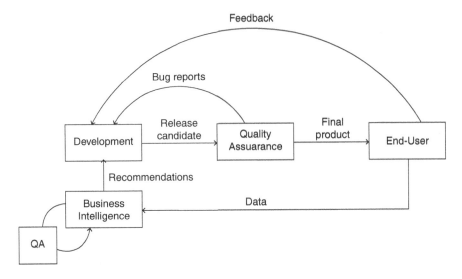

Indeed, a thorough review of data analyses, ideally with independent reproduction of key results, would likely help. What happens in practice though, is that it is very challenging to allocate resources for QA of something that does not impact the end-user (the customer) directly. We will talk about QA for data science in Part II.

While the actual impact of a flawed analysis may be comparable to that of a software bug, it will not be reported by the end-user. If a level in a game has been rendered impossible to pass because a piece of candy is forever stuck in a chocolate vortex, I, the player, will know to complain on Twitter or another forum, or to send a strongly worded letter to the customer support team. If the average conversion rate of new users has dropped by a percentage point due to a wayward recommendation from the BI team, no-one, absolutely no-one is going to be able to connect the two and demand that it be fixed.

* * *

And that, kids, is why you mustn't listen to a data scientist. That is, not until you know what they have done to avoid being wrong. And there *are* things you can do to avoid being wrong. And this is what Part II is going to be all about. But before we move on to that, let's talk about the most important—and, arguably, the most flawed—tool in data science toolbox: the human brain.

our brain sucks

Scientific method (and looking at the world as an objective reality) has been around for roughly 400 years (think Francis Bacon[1]). Philosophy and thinking about how things are—for about 2,500 years (think ancient Greeks). The human brain has been evolving for millions or even hundreds of millions of years, depending on what you consider the starting point. If we compressed time so that evolution of the brain took 24 hours, then the entire history of philosophy and science would fit in half a second, quite literally the blink of an eye.

With nearly the entire evolution of the human brain having taking place in a vastly different environment, it is only natural (quite literally) that we are good at things that were important in that environment:

- spotting ripe fruit and predators,
- reading facial expressions,
- fitting in with the tribe,

...but not so good at things that were less important:

- basing our opinion on facts,
- changing our opinion in view of new evidence,
- drawing accurate conclusions from data.

DOI: 10.1201/9781003057420-4

If you think about it, we, humans, do not really like to think. Not in the sense of casual thinking, when we are fondly remembering the sandwich we had for lunch or deciding what we are going to do after work, but in the sense of thinking about important issues, those worth having an argument about.

We identify with our ideas and our opinions. To think—really think—about them is to expose them to counterarguments and contrary evidence. To think about something you have got a strong opinion about is to voluntarily risk proving yourself wrong. And to be wrong is painful. To give up an idea with which you have associated yourself for a long time, which you have defended in many an argument, is to let something inside you die. No wonder we are not big fans of the activity.

* * *

Whether you do data science or consume its output, you would do well to recognize the quirks and limitations of the human brain, including your own. This is the case of "understanding the problem is half of the solution." You do

> You would do well to recognize the quirks and limitations of the human brain, including your own.

not need a degree in neuroscience or evolutionary psychology to deal with the most prevalent shortcomings of your cognitive process (and that degree would not necessarily help anyway):

- Correlation ≠ Causation
- Data dredging ("p-hacking")
- Cognitive biases

Let's go through these one by one.

correlation ≠ causation

"Correlation is not causation" is a phrase one can often hear these days. Definitely, if one is a data scientist. As is often the case, *knowing* a phrase does not equate *understanding* the phenomenon it describes.

Our brain is exceptionally good at seeing patterns, but not as good at correctly interpreting those found in data. There are multiple scenarios when we can see correlation between two variables that are not *causally* connected. Let's focus on the three that one can often encounter in the wild:

- reversing cause and effect,
- confounders,
- outliers.

Reversing Cause and Effect

The "easiest" way to confuse correlation with causation is when the cause and effect are reversed. A good example is the claim that tutoring makes students perform worse because they score lower on tests than their peers who are not tutored. As soon as we consider that it is underperforming students who are tutored, we can see that it is not the tutoring that causes lower test scores, but the other way around.

I have heard about a high-level meeting at one of the English Premier League clubs (not Arsenal FC, just so you know), at which a senior staff member said something to the effect of "We have crunched the data, and there is a strong correlation between players' wages and their performance. Therefore, I suggest that we pay more to our most important players."

If this sounds ridiculous, it is because it is. Without looking at the data, it is reasonable to suggest that this is another case of cause-and-effect reversal: a football player's wages do not affect his performance on the pitch, it is the performance that affects the wages.

Confounders

Confounders are arguably the most common reason that leads to correlation being mistaken for causation. A confounder is some variable Z that has an impact on both X and Y and therefore causes them to be correlated, even though neither X affects Y, nor Y affects X:

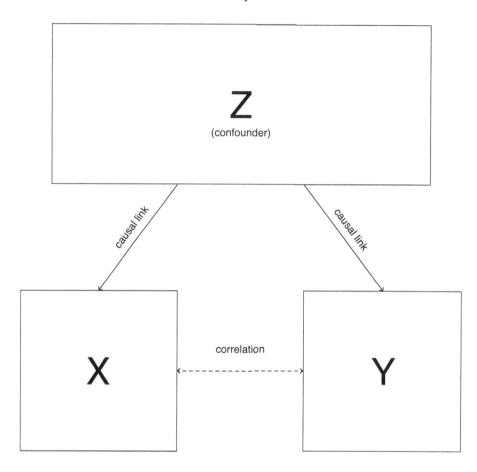

A classic example is correlation between ice-cream sales and murder rate. A direct causal link between the two makes no sense: eating ice-cream is unlikely to make you murderous, and being on either side of a murder is unlikely to make you hungry for ice-cream.

What is likely to affect both ice-cream sales and murder rate is the weather. Warm and sunny weather causes people to go outside, socialize, and buy ice-cream. With more people outside and more interaction between them, the number of murders goes up.

Outliers

Let's generate random pairs of X and Y and visualize them as a scatter plot:

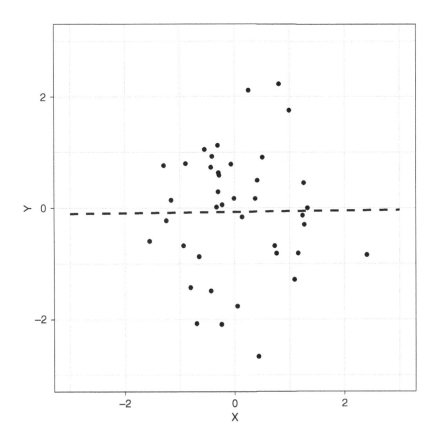

The dashed line shows the so-called linear fit. Its slope reflects the correlation between X and Y. As we can see from the plot, the linear fit is nearly horizontal, which suggests a correlation close to zero. Calculating the exact correlation between X and Y confirms it:

$$\text{cor}(X, Y) = 0.0094$$

Now, let's add an outlier—a data point residing far away from the rest:

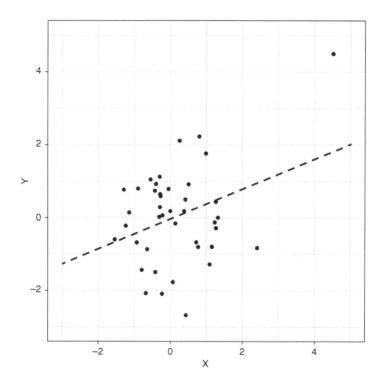

The outlier "pulls" the linear fit towards itself. With much more leverage than others, this single data point has a disproportionate impact on the correlation:

$$\text{cor}(X, Y) = 0.3458$$

The first question is if this outlier is a measurement error or a legitimate data point. If it is a measurement error, we do not need to think twice: redo the measurement or remove it from the data set.

However, not every outlier is a glitch. Real life is full of crazy outliers. These can often be observed when a metric follows a power-law distribution (one quantity varies as a power of another).

In data analysis, it is important to have an intuitive grasp of the difference between an "approximately normal" and a power-law (or similar) distribution.

Without going into too much detail, the normal distribution is characteristic of natural properties. A good example is the weight of a person. Even if we consider

It is important to have an intuitive grasp of the difference between an "approximately normal" and a power-law (or similar) distribution.

an extreme group—Japanese sumo wrestlers—most of them fall within a relatively narrow range between 70 and 180kg. If we rank them by weight, from heaviest (231.5kg) to lightest (60kg), the weight vs rank plot will look like a gentle slope with a moderate tick at either end:

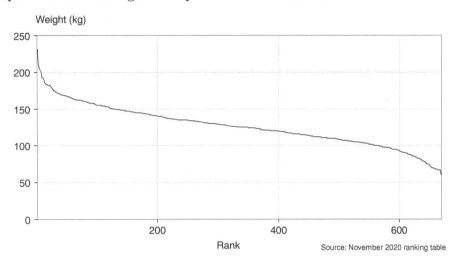

Source: November 2020 ranking table

A power-law distribution can often be found in social or economic settings. A good example is distribution of wealth. "Rich get richer." Interestingly, this principle can be applied to the very richest and still hold. If we take the list of people "worth" over 1 billion USD, the wealth vs rank plot will look very different:

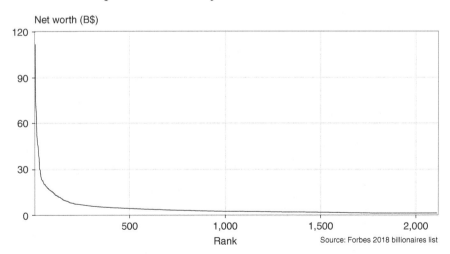

Source: Forbes 2018 billionaires list

Most of the wealth is concentrated on the left side of the plot. The top 14% of the billionaires list hold as much wealth as the remaining 86%. In comparison, in the previous example, the split would be roughly 41%–59% (i.e., the heaviest 41% would have the **same** total weight as the bottom 59%).

Power-law and similar distributions can often be seen in business (e.g., customer spend) and inevitably make the life of an analyst more difficult.

> The biggest outlier I have witnessed first-hand was a punter (someone who bets on sporting events) responsible for about half (yes, ~50%) of the bookmaker's turnover. Just imagine running an A/B test on that user base. The test group that punter got assigned to would inevitably show a much higher turnover, regardless of what the actual experiment was. Any useful signal from the A/B test would be drowned by a minor change in the mega punter's behavior.

Without going too deep into statistics, one way of dealing with heavily skewed distributions is to calculate *rank correlation*, replacing absolute values with their rank (bottom value is 1, second-bottom—2, and so on):

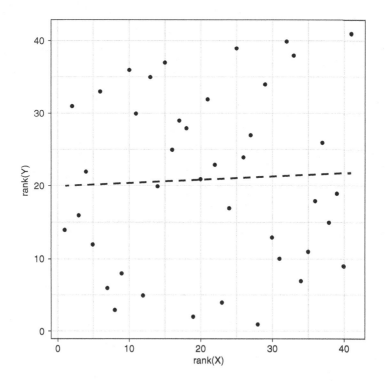

With the outlier tamed, the correlation coefficient makes more sense:

$$\text{cor}_{\text{rank}}(X, Y) = 0.0455$$

Now that you have seen *some* of the ways correlation may appear when there is no causal link between variables, I hope you will be much more skeptical when someone starts talking about correlation without any additional qualifications.

data dredging ("p-hacking")

If you look at clouds long enough, eventually one of them will look like a horse. If you burn toast every morning, eventually one of them will look like Jesus. If you look at data set after data set, eventually you will find a correlation. Not just a correlation, but a "statistically significant" correlation.

A widespread convention is to declare the results of a piece of research or an experiment "statistically significant" when the so-called "p-value" is below 0.05 or 5%. This is an arbitrary threshold, which means that, on average, 1 out of 20 "statistically significant" results will be a coincidence. If scientific journals never publish negative results, i.e., when a research does not find anything exciting, then it should not come as a surprise that a large share of *published* results are just such coincidences.

In 2015, "Five Thirty Eight" published an article titled "Science Isn't Broken,"[2] in which, among much else, they provided an interactive "p-hacking game." The goal of the game was to "discover" a statistically significant relationship between the US economy and which political party, democrats or republicans, are in office. By tweaking only a few parameters—which politicians to include, how to measure economic performance, etc.—one could obtain a p-value below 0.05 for *whichever* hypothesis they set out to prove.

To generalize from this game, any large data set can be analyzed in many different ways. The analyst can (and often has to) make multiple decisions:

- what data to include or exclude,
- what interactions between variables to consider,
- what measures to look at,
- what statistical tests to perform, etc.

"If you torture the data long enough, it will confess." (Coase, 1995) A skilled data analyst will always find a statistically significant result if they are pressed for one. It is only a matter of looking long and hard enough. Furthermore, once they have found it, they can present it to their colleagues and peer reviewers without mentioning all the data dredging it took.

Such manipulations plague so many studies that Stanford meta-science researcher John Ioannidis concluded, in his famous 2005 paper, that *most* published research findings are false. This should tell us that we must not put much trust in the "literature," i.e., even articles published in respectable scientific journals.

* * *

Let's try our hand at p-hacking. To begin, we will generate another data set with random X and Y values. Twenty observations:

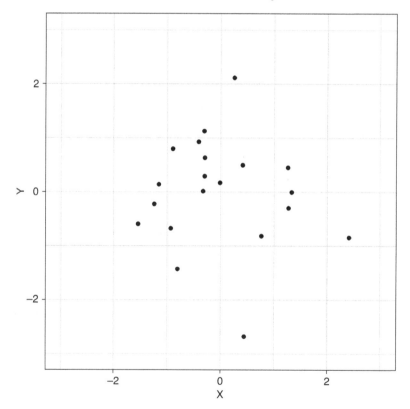

As expected, not much to write home about. It is random, and it *looks* random. Without calculating correlation, we can see that there is not much between X and Y.

But what if we generate a whole bunch of such random data sets? Let's go for a hundred:

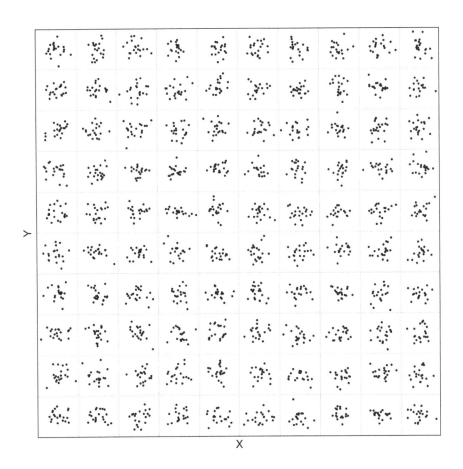

At a glance, it all still looks random. But let's find the group with strongest correlation:

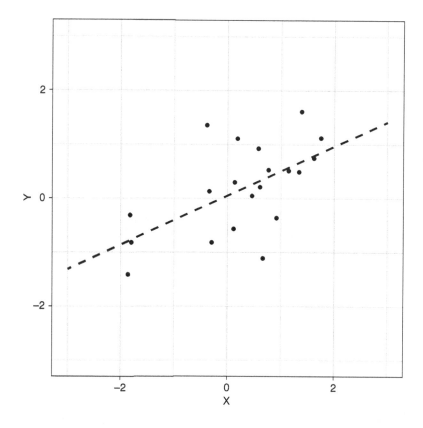

This is not a particularly strong correlation, but we can clearly see that, generally, as X increases so does Y. And just like this, we have found something "interesting" in data that was random by design. The p-value of the above linear fit is 0.00703—well below the 0.05 threshold.

If this experiment feels artificial and detached from real world...

I had to watch out for inadvertent data dredging when I was looking at correlations between players' physical load in games and their performance on various tests before and after the game.

A large number of variable combinations (e.g., 5 different load metrics × 10 different tests = 50) and relatively small data sets (e.g., 10 players × 50 games = 500) means a high chance of finding a spurious correlation.

To make matters worse, there were additional parameters that I could "play" with:

- Should we exclude data points corresponding to players who did not play the whole match? If so, what should the threshold be? 90 minutes? 75? 60?
- Given that some of the tests are isolateral (looking at right and left legs separately), should we consider left-footed players separately? What about players who are equally good with both feet?
- Similarly, should we split players by their position on the pitch: left/center/right or defense/midfield/attack?

Every split multiplies the number of theories we are testing, as well as makes the data sets even smaller.

It was possible to find a whole bunch of "statistically significant" results in that data, and even publish articles based on the analysis which, to an outsider, would look credible.

It is important to note that the chances of finding a correlation and the likely strength of that correlation increases with the number of data sets we check:

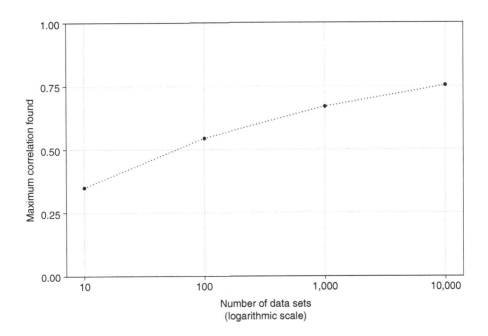

You can see that with ten data sets we should expect to find a correlation with coefficient of about 0.34 (weak), but if we somehow manage to generate 10,000 data sets, we have a decent shot at finding a correlation coefficient over 0.75 (strong).

> The more experiments you conduct and the smaller sample you use, the more likely you are to find correlation, and the stronger that correlation is likely to be.

Equally important, the likelihood and strength of a spurious correlation *decreases* if each data set is larger:

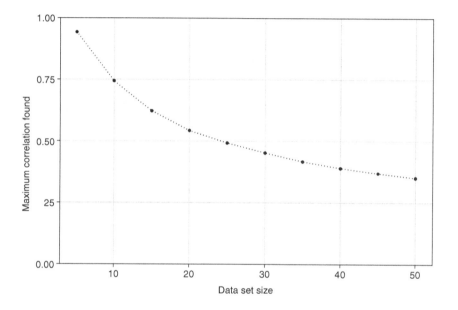

Basically, the more experiments you conduct and the smaller sample you use the more likely you are to find correlation, and the stronger that correlation is likely to be.

cognitive biases

If our goal is to obtain truth, which hopefully it is, then cognitive biases are a certain type of obstacles to that goal. Not every obstacle is a bias, but any bias is an obstacle. A systematic deviation from the rational judgment, a bias makes us stray away from the path, distorts our worldview, and pushes us towards suboptimal decisions.

The Wikipedia page on cognitive biases[3] lists about 200 (!) of them. This calls for a "less is more" approach. Listing all the ways your brain can trick you is less likely to help you and more likely to leave you confused and catatonic. A sensible approach is to focus on, you guessed it, the three most common biases you are likely to encounter when people use data:

- confirmation bias, when one makes a decision before they have seen the data;
- optimism bias, when one suppresses their doubts;
- information bias, when one seeks information that will not affect their action.

Let's explore these in more detail.

Confirmation Bias

"Everything you look for and all that you perceive has a way of proving whatever you believe."

This is one of the more well-known biases. It makes us collect and interpret data in favor of own belief or hypothesis. The danger is two-fold:

- We can focus on the data that is likely to support what we already believe and ignore the data that is likely to prove us wrong.
- Even when looking at the same data, we can interpret it differently based on our pre-existing beliefs.

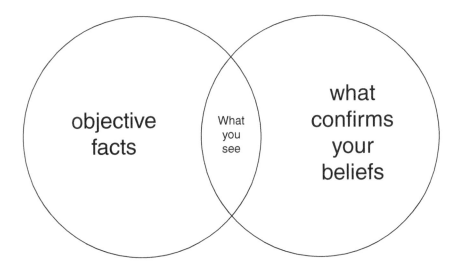

Confirmation bias pervades both hard and soft sciences. Data science is no exception. They do not say it out loud, but most people do not want data, they want confirmation of what they are already thinking. Depending on the phase of a data science project, confirmation bias can manifest in various forms:

> Most people do not want data, they want confirmation of what they are already thinking.

- **Before the project even begins**:

    The data scientist receives "loaded" questions:

    "Can we find evidence that...?"

    "How can we show that...?"

- **Once the initial results are in**:

    Data dredging is invited to the party:

    "What if we only look at the last year and exclude high spenders?"

- **Presentation**:

    Results are presented and/or interpreted in a way that makes it look like they support the original hypothesis, ignoring the bits that do not quite fit.

One way to fight confirmation bias is to introduce a structured and consistent process that leaves less room for it to play a role.

When it comes to academic research, one way to improve the quality of scientific studies that has been getting traction is to have scientists pre-register their studies.

In traditional research publishing, a paper is peer-reviewed only after the study has been completed. A registered report is reviewed *before* the scientist collects data. If the research question and methods are deemed sound, the author is offered "in-principle acceptance" of the paper, which practically guarantees publication, regardless of the results. This also helps with publication bias, when only "interesting" results are published, which can easily skew the true picture.

In case of data science in a business setting, this approach may come across as an overkill. The main challenge will be convincing people that the extra burden of reviewing data analyses prior to carrying them out is worth it. However, a scaled-down version may well be a possibility.

The first step is to ensure that all data analytics requests are phrased as a neutral question and never an objective.

- **Bad**: Can we find data that proves that making our players do high-intensity runs on the day before a game hurts their performance in the game?
- **Better**: Can we measure correlation between pre-game training intensity and in-game outputs?

Instead of a formal pre-registration process, it may be enough to simply write down the analysis question, what is going to be measured, and how the conclusion will be drawn and email it to all relevant parties. This can easily prove the data scientist's most usefully spent 5 minutes.

Pre-registering analyses may not completely eliminate loaded questions and biased presentation of the results. But we should try and make torturing data as conspicuous and difficult as possible.

Optimism Bias

In his seminal book *Thinking, Fast and Slow* (2012), Kahneman says that optimism bias "may well be the most significant of the cognitive biases." This bias generates the illusion that we have substantial control over our lives.

One kind of unwarranted optimism, the so-called planning fallacy is the tendency to overestimate benefits and underestimate costs, impelling people to take on risky projects. In 2002, American kitchen remodeling was expected on average to cost $18,658, but actually cost $38,769 (Holt, 2011).

To explain such overconfidence, Kahneman introduced the concept of "What You See Is All There Is": when the mind makes decisions, it deals primarily with "known knowns," what it has already observed, and rarely considers "known unknowns," what is relevant but about which it has no information. As for "unknown unknowns," the mind appears completely oblivious to the possibility of their existence.

An interesting feature of optimism bias is that it tends to get stronger the more people you have got in the room. When we are on our own, those of us who are of a more pessimistic nature often have doubts as to whether something is a good idea or whether a project is likely to succeed. But as soon as we find ourselves in the company of others, even just one person, we also find it harder to bring up the "negative" thoughts.

A great example is provided by people who are getting married, and who estimate the likelihood of their divorce as negligible, despite the average divorce rate being around 50% (in the Western World).

Any serious project, including those in data science, brings together a number of people. In a project meeting, everyone feels better talking about how the project is going to succeed than about how it can get derailed. We do not like nay-sayers, and we do not like being one. While it might be beneficial *for the project* if someone mentioned a potential problem, it may be not beneficial for that someone personally. A Nash equilibrium of ignoring the elephant in the room is achieved.

I spent a lot of time working on optimizing levels in *Candy Crush*.

When it comes to a *Candy Crush* level, you do not want it to be too easy, otherwise the player will just breeze through it. Neither will they enjoy passing the level, nor have any incentive to make an in-game purchase (e.g., a so-called "booster," that can make it easier to beat a level). You do not want the level to be too hard either, as some players will simply give up on the game altogether ("churn" in business-speak). You want to hit the sweet spot, so that most players pass the level after a reasonable number of attempts, which will give them a dopamine kick as well as a chance to spend money should they feel like getting a leg up.

We would identify levels that had a poor monetization-to-churn ratio and ask level designers to create a few alternative versions. We would then run an A/B test and compare the performance of these new versions against the original. Typically, at least one of the alternative versions would show a significant—in the area of 10%—increase in revenue per player, so we would replace the original level and happily report the positive impact on the business.

Everyone was content with the procedure, and no-one asked inconvenient questions about variance, confidence intervals, statistical significance, etc.

The bitter truth became difficult to ignore when we had accidentally run an "A/A test," with two groups of players served the same version of the level. The difference in revenue per player was about 11%, i.e., comparable to what we would normally consider an indisputable success. Of course, in this scenario, it showed that the metric was too volatile, and a 10% difference could be due to chance. A simulation we ran afterwards showed that we would need a difference of at least 20% to conclude with confidence that one version of a level was more profitable than another (given the typical number of players and duration of the A/B test).

Arguably, a more important lesson was that even if you have got a group of numerate data scientists and businesspeople, the optimism bias can lead to everyone overlooking problems that are obvious in hindsight.

You cannot fight optimism bias without making it okay to sound pessimistic. (Not to *be* pessimistic, that is very difficult, but to *sound* pessimistic, which only takes being less optimistic than everyone else.) It is a rare environment in which one feels comfortable coming across as a nay-sayer. There is a reason people campaign under "Yes, we can" and not under "Hmm... I am not quite sure about this."

> You cannot fight optimism bias without making it okay to sound pessimistic.

To counter optimism bias, we need to greet every idea with the question "What can possibly go wrong?"—and not in its usual rhetorical form. When applied to project planning, this can be formalized as the technique known as "project pre-mortem."

You may be familiar with the concept of project post-mortem. In the business context, this is a project meeting that happens once the project is over. If the project has failed, the team will discuss why it happened. Both failure and success may present valuable lessons.

A project pre-mortem comes at the beginning of a project. Its key feature is that the discussion takes place under the assumption that the project *has* failed, and all the team can do now is to understand why. Instead of "What might go wrong?" the question becomes "What *did* go wrong?" This makes a big difference: prospective hindsight—imagining that an event has already occurred—increases the ability to correctly identify reasons for future outcomes by 30% (Klein, 2007).

Information Bias

This bias makes us seek information when it will not affect our action. While it sounds like it is relatively harmless, it nonetheless has negative consequences.

We, people, are curious creatures. It varies from person to person, but as a species we like novelty, the feeling of discovery, figuring stuff out. We just need to know. This is one of our greatest qualities,

> In the context of data science, more data is not always better.

but, left unchecked, it can have a detrimental effect on our decision-making. In the context of data science, more data is not always better.

Seeking more data without a good reason can have a negative impact in different ways:

- more work,
- diluted argument,
- lost purpose.

More Work

The obvious negative impact of seeking more data is that it requires more work. While this is painfully obvious to the person doing the work, it may be easily—both in the sense of "likely" and "comfortably"—overlooked by others.

> There is often an inverse correlation between how simple a question sounds and how simple it is to answer.

There is often an inverse correlation between how simple a question sounds and how simple it is to answer.

"What is the correlation between the distance a player covers in a game, relative to his season average, and the height of his standing vertical jump measured next day, again, relative to his season average?" may sound so very complicated, but if the required data is available, it is likely to be a quick, do-it-before-lunch job.

"Does running more help us win games?" may sound like a straightforward question to a football coach, but one can write a PhD thesis and still not produce a satisfying answer.

> A good data scientist keeps the quantity of information down but drives the quality of information up.

Human curiosity is forever pushing us to ask for more and more data. It is the responsibility of the data scientist to apply pressure in the opposite direction.

A good data scientist keeps the quantity of information down but drives the quality of information up.

Diluted Argument

The less obvious negative impact of seeking more data is that it dilutes the argument.

In Chapter 1, we discussed that, unless data science is the product, its end goal is to change opinions. This implies a debate, either an actual debate or a one-way discussion, e.g., via a report. If you pay attention when you are having an argument, you may have noticed that you are more likely to make a strong case if you limit yourself to one or two most important points.

Whenever someone gives you multiple reasons for their decision, it is unlikely that the real reason is among them.

- Why aren't you coming to the gym today?
- Well... I am really busy at work these days, and I think the gym's going to be crowded; also, I need to do my laundry, and my back has been playing up recently...

The list of reasons may go on, but you probably know that the actual reason is a simple "I do not want to." All other reasons are *excuses*.

In theory, making the right decision requires taking into account many different factors. In machine learning, the more meaningful factors (independent variables, "features") you can generate, the more accurate predictions you will get. But even then, as the number of features grow, you are likely to observe the "Pareto principle," when a small subset of features drives the lion's share of the model's predictive power. For example, when trying to predict if a football player is going to sustain a non-impact injury, you will probably see that the most important variables are match and training workload, and history of previous injuries. At the same time, adding data on weather conditions and what boots the player wore does not yield higher prediction accuracy. That is, "more" does not produce "better."

In practice, when decisions are made by people, "more" (data) often results in "worse" (decisions). Unlike machine learning models, we are not good at adding up evidence. We do not

> We, people, are very good at forming opinions based on little to no data.

intuitively understand the weight of each factor, how much they tip the scale, and how confident we should be that it is A and not B. We, people, are very good at forming opinions based on little to no data. The tiniest shred of evidence in favor of an alternative hypothesis can tip the scales—more so if the confirmation bias is at play.

Any discussion worth having will have arguments for and against. The more numbers and plots you hoard, regardless of their pertinence, the more you risk losing clarity and focus:

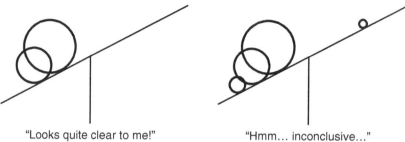

"Looks quite clear to me!"   "Hmm... inconclusive..."

If you can always find *some* evidence either for or against a hypothesis, you will always have to go back to square one: what your intuition tells you. So much for data science.

* * *

The solution to information bias is as follows: decide what you are going to look at and how you are going to make your decision *before* the analysis. Focus on 2–3 most important, most intuitive metrics and declare loud and clear what your decision process is going to be:

Bad	Better
Decision maker [DM]: We have implemented this cool new feature. Let's run an A/B test!...	Decision maker [DM]: We have implemented this cool new feature. Let's run an A/B test!...
Data scientist [DS]: No impact on revenue compared to the control group.	Data scientist [DS]: What do we want to look at, and how are we going to make the decision?
DM: Hmm... But it is such a cool feature... What if we segment users and look at each segment separately?	DM: This feature is primarily targeted at high spenders. Can we look at them separately in addition to the entire user base? If the 80% confidence interval for the change in revenue is above zero, we will roll it out.
DS: Still nothing.	
DM: Hmm... What about conversion rate for users who signed up during the first week of the A/B test?...	DS: No impact on total revenue. The 80% confidence interval for high spenders is −2% + 5%.DM: Oh, well, back to the drawing board.
DS: Low and high spenders appear to spend slightly less, but those in the middle may have been spending slightly more than in the control group...	
DM: Excellent, let's roll it out to the medium segment! *(Open PowerPoint.)*	

An important exception to the above rule is *exploratory analysis*. When you do not know anything yet, it is too early to start thinking about how you are going to be making decisions. This is the wonderful time of asking questions:

- How many users have we got?
- What do they do with our app?
- How many of them pay?
- What is the spend distribution look like?

But once you have figured where you are and where you want to go, you would better decide how you are going to measure your progress and not change the rules whenever it suits you.

Lost Purpose

Looking for more data can make you lose sight of the original goal. I heard a memorable formulation of this principle from someone who had been involved in the training process of a rowing team. In a nutshell, any idea would be greeted with a simple question: "Will it make the boat go faster?"

A sport like rowing has a pleasant one-dimensionality to it. If something helps you shave a few seconds off of your time, it is worth your trouble, and vice versa. In a sport like football, where the result on any given day depends on a multitude of factors *and luck*, people try to move the needle even a tiny bit doing all kinds of things, which makes it much harder to keep in mind how it is all connected to the coveted W.

For example: win next game ← keep players match-fit ← prevent players from getting injured ← avoid spikes in training load ← daily report that shows each player's day-to-day training load + training session planning tool that forecasts training load, so that we can make sure that every player gets the volume they need.

In this example, the daily report and planning tool are clearly connected to the ultimate goal, even if indirectly. A common temptation is to start building all kinds of reports, tools, and colorful dashboards, which may make it look like you are "leveraging" your data, but in reality is more likely to make it harder to focus on what matters.

Whenever I am asked to do something or have what feels like a brilliant idea, I try to stop and ask myself, "Will it make the boat go faster?"

glossary

Nash equilibrium (game theory) is achieved when no player can benefit by changing strategies while the other players keep theirs unchanged.

P-value is the probability of obtaining results at least as extreme as the results actually observed, assuming that the "null hypothesis" (e.g., "There is no correlation between X and Y") is true.

Spurious correlation is a correlation between variables that are not causally linked, due to coincidence or a confounding factor.

works cited

Essays on Economics and Economists / Ronald H. Coase / 1995 University of Chicago Press.

Performing a project premortem / Gary Klein / *Harvard Business Review* (September 2007).

Thinking, Fast and Slow / Daniel Kahneman / 2012 Penguin.

Two Brains Running / Jim Holt / *The New York Times* (November 2011).

"Why Most Published Research Findings are False" / John P. A. Ioannidis / 2005 *PLoS Med* 2(8): e124.

notes

1 An English philosopher and statesman, who has been called the father of empiricism.

2 https://fivethirtyeight.com/features/science-isnt-broken/.

3 https://en.wikipedia.org/wiki/List_of_cognitive_biases. Last edited on July 14, 2021.

II

a new hope

Just because data science is hard, and our brain was not exactly designed to do it we should not stop trying our best. The hype around data science is not entirely unfounded. When done right, it can, indeed, transform businesses and disrupt industries (and even create new ones). "When" is the operative word here.

There is lot of the material on how to do data science the right way that falls into two categories:

- Articles full of truisms, such as "Data quality is important," which you cannot and will not argue with, but which leave you none the wiser as to how to actually do things better.
- Books and workshops on tools and workflows that enable one to do data analysis, but do not necessarily cover the chasm between using a tool and achieving the desired result.

This book tries to fill in the blanks. Online courses and bootcamps can prepare you for the role of a junior data scientist; saying things like "Deliver relevant results" and "Empower business stakeholders" may work when interviewing for a managerial position; but we will focus on the stuff in between—the magical transformation of data science efforts into something useful.

This part of the book will deal with three major areas:

- data science for people, not for its own sake (doing the right thing),
- quality assurance (doing it correctly),
- automation (never having to do it again).

DOI: 10.1201/9781003057420-5

It will all be essentially about data science best practices.

Just like any best practices, rules of thumb and other kinds of guidelines, data science best practices do not emerge from nowhere. It is important to understand that the process is as follows:

1. Practitioners try to solve a certain problem.
2. Some approaches work better than others.
3. Success and failure stories are distilled into dos and don'ts— a best practice is born.

When writing about best practices, it is difficult to avoid words like "should" and "must." The reader would do well to remember that there are no sacred texts in data science. And even if there were, this would not be one of them.

"Should" and "must" are only convenient shortcuts. "Thou shalt not lie" is easier to say and remember than "Telling lies is detrimental to one's character and destroys mutual trust, which is a crucial resource for a group of people with a shared goal." Similarly, "Always comment your code" is a shortcut for "Commenting your code will make it easier for you and others to maintain it and, if necessary, reuse it in the future."

If someone tells you that you should do this, or that you must never do that, and you are not sure where they are coming from, it is a good idea to ask: "What will happen if I do? What if I don't?" Writing about best practices, I will try to make it clear what good things will happen if you follow it, and what bad things will happen if you don't.

There are no hard rules beyond the laws of physics (and even they are just our best guess for the moment), but experience shows that it is better to start out with known best practices and only deviate from them once you know the ins and outs.

data science for people

When discussing data science best practices, it is important to note that there is a hierarchy to them. A best practice never exists without context, and for it to make sense, it may be required that a more high-level best practice (or several) has been put in place.

For example, there is no point in arguing which machine learning technique to use if the data the model will be trained on is rubbish. Thus, data-related best practices come before those specific to machine learning. Improving the data will have a bigger impact on the model accuracy than picking a more sophisticated machine learning algorithm.

This chapter will attempt to outline the most general of data science best practices in a meaningful order:

1. Align data science efforts with business needs.

2. Mind data science hierarchy of needs.

3. Make it simple, reproducible, and shareable.

I do not know about you, but when I am looking at these I cannot help thinking, "Aren't they all extremely obvious?" Who does not want to align data science efforts with business needs? Who wants to make it unnecessarily complicated? Who does not want to automate everything that can be automated, and save time and money? But then, if these principles were adhered to by—not even all—most organizations, I would not feel the urge to write this book in the first place.

Let's go through these best practices one by one and try to understand why they are ignored more often than not.

DOI: 10.1201/9781003057420-6

align data science efforts with business needs

In any organization that aspires to be data-driven, the first thing to look at is the alignment of data science efforts with business needs. This may sound obvious, but I have been in and observed situations when data science efforts were primarily driven not by what the business *needed*, but by one or both of the following two:

- what data scientists *wanted* to do,
- what people working with data scientists *thought* the business needed.

Let's address the first one: data scientists doing what they want rather than what business needs.

As science is concerned with seeking truth, data science is concerned with seeking truth in data. The two main reasons to seek truth are:

1. **Curiosity**: you want to understand something for the sake of understanding. This is what often drives data scientists. They want to do an exploratory analysis, run an A/B test or master a new tool not because it will necessarily create business value, but simply because they are curious.
2. **Pragmatism**: whatever your goal, you can get closer to it by better understanding the domain. In case of a business, you may, for example, hope to increase revenue by better understanding your customers' needs and behaviors.

A fundamental challenge of creating a data-driven organization is the marriage of these two: curious people working towards pragmatic goals. The optimal proportion of curiosity and pragmatism will vary from company to company. A research data scientist working on pushing the boundaries of deep learning may do well to be 95% curious and 5% pragmatic, whereas a business analyst supporting a small chain of retail stores is likely to benefit from being only 5% curious and 95% pragmatic. Data analysts in most companies will be at their most productive when combining curiosity and pragmatism in reasonable proportions.

The absolute majority of data analysts I have had the privilege to work with had enough curiosity for two people. Some would be more interested in statistical analysis, some—in writing efficient code, others—in building data pipelines, but all of them would have a pre-existing interest in doing something data-related for its own sake.

The same could not be said about every analyst's passion for meeting quarterly business objectives. Most of them, especially those just breaking into the field, would look for an interesting project first and think about its value for the business later, if ever. Whereas in the ideal world it would be the other way around.

This challenge is best addressed top down: a business-minded data science team manager will have a shot at aligning less business-minded data scientists and making sure they deliver business value. It is difficult to imagine a bottom-up approach to be successful.

I have personally worked with a variety of data science managers, with widely varying degrees of business-mindedness and tech-savviness. My experience is that a manager who understands business needs but knows nothing about data science will generally outperform a tech-savvy manager of comparable general intelligence who has lost touch with business goals.

> A manager who understands business needs but knows nothing about data science will generally outperform a tech-savvy manager of comparable general intelligence who has lost touch with business goals.

In a smaller data science organization, it can be the data scientist themselves who determine the overall direction of research.

I once got a question from a data analyst who had just joined a sports club. He wanted my input on how to start off with the data and what questions he should be looking to answer.

While I did my best to answer in a friendly and constructive manner, I could not help thinking, "I am not the person you should be talking to. Your job is to help people running the club. Ask *them* what they need, not me."

For a data scientist, it may be useful to know what your peers in other companies work on. If they happen to have solved a problem similar to one you are working on, you may be able to learn from their experience (and you can certainly learn from their mistakes). However, at the end of the day, everything you do you do in the context of your organization, and you are best positioned to find out what needs to be done. And it is arguably the most important part of your job. You cannot outsource understanding the needs of the business.

> You cannot outsource understanding the needs of the business.

One well-known management methodology that can help align what the data science team does with what business needs is objectives and key results (OKR). The idea behind this goal-setting framework, popularized by Google, is to ensure that the company focuses efforts on the same important issues throughout the organization. When OKR is applied correctly, anything a data scientist (or any employee, for that matter) does should be connected to an overarching company's objective. Conversely, if a task cannot be connected to such objective, it can and should be dropped.

Unfortunately, as often happens with methodologies and frameworks, they can be applied in theory while very much ignored in practice. A certain kind of cargo cult takes place: meetings are held, presentations are shown around, to-do lists are created, but when the dust settles, it is business as usual, with people doing what they have always been doing.

> Without a change in organization culture and everyone's mindset, a management framework is just a yoga mat that was bought and put away in the loft.

Without a change in organization culture and everyone's mindset, a management framework is just a yoga mat that was bought and put away in the loft.

* * *

What if the data scientists are happy to work on whatever can make the biggest impact on the bottom line, but are being asked to deliver projects with a questionable connection to business? This can easily happen in a large organization with a thick layer of middle management, but smaller companies are not exempt from this risk either.

This problem is exacerbated by the old adage, "Easier said than done." When an idea is born at the higher level of organization, it is easy to (1) keep it vague, so it is not immediately obvious whether or not it is pertinent to business goals, and (2) ignore the opportunity cost, i.e., that getting something done means that something else does not get done.

If wasting resources on a useless project is a crime, then working on such project is being an accomplice. "I was told to do it by my manager," is an excuse which will not give you back the wasted time. If you do not know why you are doing something, you are probably wasting your time.

> If you do not know why you are doing something, you are probably wasting your time.

* * *

If you remember the underpants-stealing gnomes from Part I, a data science project is usually described as phase 1 (collect underpants) with an implied phase 3 (profit). It is your job to find out what phase 2 is. If it is there at all.

A great technique to find something out is: to ask questions.

It takes practice to ask questions without annoying the hell out of the other person, but even if you are new at it, it is better to be annoying for 5 minutes than to waste 5 months on something nobody needs.

> It is better to be annoying for five minutes than to waste five months on something nobody needs.

For example, let's imagine a marketing manager (MM) who wants a data scientist (DS) to create a "churn" prediction model—a machine learning algorithm that predicts, with some accuracy, whether or not a player is about to quit the game and never come back:

MM: Let's create a player churn prediction model.
DS: What for? (The questions can and probably should be phrased more diplomatically in real life, but here we can keep them blunt for the sake of brevity.)
MM: So that we can predict if a player is likely to leave the game and never come back.
DS: What for?
MM: So that we can try and keep them in the game.
DS: How?
MM: Hmm... We could give them an in-game gift or something...
DS: So, we would need to make a prediction in real time, while they are in the game, so that they will see the gift?

Already after three open-ended questions, they are discussing what exactly has to happen for the project to be successful—what is in phase 2 that will connect phase 1 (churn prediction model) with phase 3 (fewer players leaving the game).

This is similar to a well-known technique of "Five whys," first used by Toyota Motor Corporation. I find that a data scientist can usually make do with the "Three what for's" variation.

This technique may require that the person asking questions with the insistence of a 4-year-old feel safe in doing so. That takes a certain company culture and/or personal relationship with one's stakeholders. A more subtle approach, which does not put the data scientist in a confrontational position, is to get working without asking too many questions, but focus on rapid prototyping and getting feedback as early as possible.

Let's say an important person with low tolerance for challenging questions asks you to put together an interactive report, where they will be able to select this and that, and also with filters, and so that they see different metrics, and they can click on anything and boom!—another page opens and...

You could roll up your sleeves, get your head down, and deliver your best approximation of the above in a few weeks or even months, with the hope that the important person still wants the thing they were one day so enthusiastic about. Or—you could create the simplest prototype imaginable, let's say, a rough mock-up of the user interface sloppily hand-drawn in a graphics editor, with a static plot showing one possible view of the report—all done in half an hour—and show it to the important person while the memory of the conversation is still fresh, and ask them if this is what they had in mind. You would find yourself in one of the following situations:

- "Yes, spot on!"—All right, they seem to really want *that*. You should better start working on the interactive report in earnest, but it is still a good idea to show them what you have got a few days in.

- "Yeah, but not exactly what I was thinking..."—Good, this is a discussion now. You will be able to correct your course, and you *definitely* should come back as soon as you have got an updated prototype.

- "Hmm... let me think about it."—Now that the important person is looking at something more tangible rather than a prettily vague idea in their head, they may cool off the latter, or at least have a proper think about what they *actually* want. Good job you have not spent weeks or months trying to implement the original blurry vision.

* * *

Aligning a data science team with the rest of the organization is not something you do once. The entropy goes up, things fall apart, and people forget why they are doing what they are doing. It takes constant effort to keep a business running, and it takes constant effort to make sure data science stays relevant.

> It takes constant effort to make sure data science stays relevant.

mind data science hierarchy of needs

The alignment of data science efforts with business needs is, as they say, necessary but not sufficient for success. When something can hypothetically have a positive impact on the business, it does not necessarily follow that you should start working on it right now.

You may be familiar with Maslow's hierarchy of needs or, simply, Maslow's pyramid:

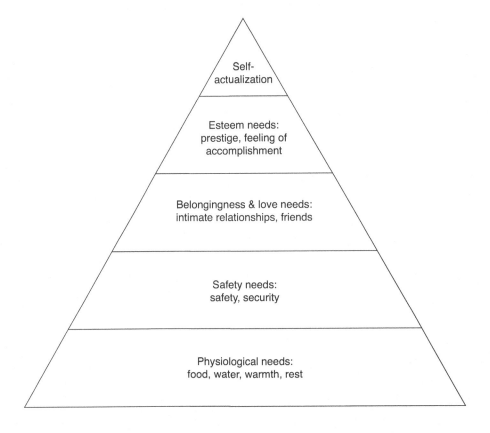

What the pyramid tells us, in a nutshell, is that one cannot worry about a higher level until the levels below have been satisfied. A hungry person without shelter will not concern themselves with self-actualization. Maslow's pyramid is self-evident to anyone who has had to struggle upwards from the bottom level.

A similar pyramid can be drawn for data science:

Just like Maslow's pyramid, this one has got a self-evident look. It would be difficult to argue against that you need to collect data before you can store it, and that you need to store it before you can explore it, and so on.

I have been in a meeting with top managers of a respectable medium-size company, which was only beginning to catch up with regards to using the data of its massive user base. In the data science hierarchy of needs, the company was still muddling through the second level from the bottom: *some* data was being collected and stored in a database that had signs of "organic growth"—disparate tables, columns added ad hoc by software developers, rudimentary documentation put together by some who cared more than others...

The company could not yet boast comprehensive data-driven business reports or A/B testing, yet the managers kept repeating the phrase "leapfrog to AI." They were very enthusiastic about skipping half the pyramid, although they would not and could not go into detail of how exactly they envisioned doing so.

Using the analogy with Maslow's pyramid, they were akin to someone being chased by a bear in the woods yet thinking about how best to optimize their investment portfolio.

First things first.

The data science hierarchy of needs does not imply that you have to build a perfect data infrastructure before you can do any data analysis. You will do better to start with a narrow sliver across several layers and then expand horizontally. For example, if you are monetizing

> The data science hierarchy of needs does not imply that you have to build a perfect data infrastructure before you can do any data analysis.

a web application, your first foray into data science can go as follows:

1. **Collect**: log financial transactions.

2. **Store**: save information such as timestamp and amount of transaction to a database. You can plan ahead and also save things like what the customer paid for, in which part of the app, device, browser, language, etc.

3. **Explore**: verify the data being collected against your financial records—does everything add up? Is there anything that looks off? Already at this step you can make an interesting discovery or two.

4. **Aggregate**: create a simple report that allows you to plot revenue as time series—you can already see trends and periodic cycles. Add the option of splitting revenue by product, country, and so on—and you can get a lot of insights into what is going on with the business.

Without doing anything sophisticated (the above will not necessarily require even hiring a data engineer/analyst), you will have cut through the first four levels of the pyramid and got a much deeper understanding of the business.

As a rule of thumb, it is best to go for the low-hanging fruit first. An automatic alert when the number of transactions per hour drops below a threshold can be a very simple, borderline boring thing to implement, but it can save you days' worth of revenue when a routine update accidentally removes the "Buy" button. On the contrary, using machine learning to predict what a user may be interested in and provide them with personalized recommendations makes for a cool data science project, but it takes much more time and effort to implement and its impact may prove negligible.

Low-hanging fruit is the sweetest.

make it simple, reproducible, and shareable

Now that you have made sure that you are doing what the business needs, and that you are starting with what it needs first and foremost, we come to the third fundamental best practice—or, rather, a set of three values. These values are simplicity, reproducibility, and shareability.

Failing to uphold these values will not necessarily render your work useless or insufficient. Yet, if you notice that you work is lacking any of them, you will do well to ask yourself why.

Simple

The value, and even beauty, of simplicity have always been talked about. "Perfection is achieved, not when there is nothing more to add, but when there is nothing left to take away" was written by Antoine de Saint-Exupéry in the 1940s. The less flowery "Keep it simple, stupid" has been with us since 1960. Yet even a cursory glance will reveal a lot of unnecessary complexity around us. Just look at a TV remote.

There are three main reasons behind the proliferation of unnecessary complexity.

First, simplicity is often perceived as a shortcoming, as a lack of sophistication. We do not want to come across as *simple*tons. Especially at work. Especially if we are supposed to be a data *scientist*, someone who may be expected to be equally good at fixing a broken MacBook and hacking a Pentagon server.

Enter smoke and mirrors. If people do not quite understand what you are talking about, they may think you are clever and brilliant. Use long words and talk at least one level above that of your audience. Do they understand "mean" and "median"? Throw in "p-value" and "null hypothesis." They understand these as well? Mention "log-normal distribution" and "non-parametric correlation." The less they understand, the cleverer you look.

When I used to share a small office with a few non-technical people, whenever I wanted to take a break without making it obvious, I would open a Linux console (that black screen with a lot of gibberish and a blinking cursor you see in a movie about computer hackers) on one of my two monitors.

Even though that black screen with a few lines of incomprehensible text would be just sitting there, my colleagues did not *understand* it, and it was easy for them to assume that something magical was happening.

Second, simplicity does not have a constituency in the same way complexity usually does. The latter grows as various features are added to the product, e.g., a data-driven report. Every feature has a constituency—a group of people who want it, who expect to benefit from it, who can argue for it to be added. As for simplicity, it is a non-excludable good. Everyone benefits from it, but rarely in an immediately obvious way. This is why there are almost always more people arguing for adding a feature than against it. Features are added one after another. The complexity grows. Everyone is suffering from the "feature bloat," but there is no will or effort to push back.

Last but not least, even when we *want* to keep it simple, it is often surprisingly hard. Recent research has shown that people consistently consider changes that add components over those that subtract them (Adams et al., 2021). Whenever we have got a difficult problem to solve, we rarely come up with the simplest solution possible. If we know what we are doing, we come up with *a* solution, which is usually quite complicated. To make it simpler, to take away anything that is not absolutely needed, we have to understand the problem really well, and to explore a multitude of possible solutions, most of which will not be obvious.

This immediately brings to mind the data-ink ratio concept introduced by Edward Tufte, probably the best-known expert on data visualization, in his *The Visual Display of Quantitative Data* (1983): "A large share of ink on a graphic should present data-information, the ink changing as the data change. Data-ink is the non-erasable core of a graphic, the non-redundant ink arranged in response to variation in the numbers represented."

This principle of "less is more" does not end with data visualization. Programming code also lends itself nicely to decluttering. As the saying goes, "Good programmers write good code. Great programmers write no code. Zen programmers delete code." Almost without exception, whenever I go back to code I wrote even just a few months ago, my reaction is "Oh my... why did I make it so complicated?!" A recent example is a web dashboard that tracks the physical output of football players during game (with real-time data being fed into it). The original version had close to 600 lines of code and was very clunky. The new one, that I built knowing what really matters and what is deadwood, is under 200 lines of code and, as a bonus, works beautifully both on a large screen and on a mobile device.

* * *

Keeping things simple has two benefits. First, it makes it easier to maintain, fix, and change things further down the road. This is often underappreciated, especially when something is being built to a tight deadline. "Just get it done, we will polish it later" invariably turns out to be wishful thinking.

Second, the simpler the thing, the easier it is to explain and to use. Again, this is often underappreciated, especially when something is built for less tech-savvy users. For example, when it comes to data visualization, I have explored the entire spectrum from a plain bar chart to an animated chord diagram. No end-user has ever complained about a bar chart (this is not to say that making a good bar chart is trivial), while the animated chord diagram drew a few ah's and ooh's, but did not find a practical use.

You do not have to justify something being simple, but you need a very good reason for something to be complicated.

> You do not have to justify something being simple, but you need a very good reason for something to be complicated.

Reproducible

If you have been successful in aligning data science with business needs, you may find yourself very popular. Your colleagues from different areas of the business will flock to you to unlock the power of data analysis and data visualization. And this is good.

This is good, but it forces you into a difficult trade-off: try and help as many people as you can by doing things the "quick and dirty" way or refuse to lower your standards and have to say no to less important or urgent requests.

It is tempting to move quickly and take shortcuts. You get a straightforward question from marketing department, find a data set, and whip up a script that spits out a few numbers. Excellent—email them over and move on to the next request. It takes zero effort to decide that certain things either do not need to be done or do not need to be done *right away*:

- quality assurance (extensively covered in the next chapter),
- source control (the practice of tracking changes to programming code),
- documentation and/or comments in the code,
- making sure the analysis is self-contained.

Skipping the above may feel like a viable (or even *the only* viable) strategy in the short term—after all, you are delivering results—but you are unlikely to get away with it in the long run. (Whether or not you or anyone else will realize it is a separate question.)

A request from an external stakeholder can often appear to be a one-off event, something that can be dealt with quickly and forever forgotten, but in reality you will probably have to go back to your solution, and probably more than once, for various reasons:

- A mistake has been found in the results, and you need to comb through your analysis and fix it.
- You have got a follow-up question or a request to extend the analysis.
- The stakeholders want the analysis to be done on a monthly basis, or even better, made available as a self-service report.

It is not so bad if the above happens soon after you have dealt with the original request. You have no trouble locating the data you used and the script you wrote. You still remember why you chose this particular approach and what exactly different bits of the code do. It can be much worse if you have to go back after a few weeks or months. Can you find your script? Can you still run it, or are you getting error messages because you have updated various libraries and packages it uses? Is the data you used still there? Is it the same data or has it changed? Can you verify that the script produces the same results before you make any changes? Do you already feel that it may be easier to do everything from scratch?

And this is reproducing an analysis *you* did. What if you need to reproduce one that was done by another data scientist? A data scientist who has left the company? Does anyone know where they stored their scripts? Which one is the one you are looking for? Why doesn't it run on your laptop? Now you definitely feel it will be easier to do everything from scratch.

This kind of struggle when an analysis has been done with no thought for reproducibility is only half of the problem. If external stakeholders realize that a piece of analysis cannot be reproduced, it will undermine the credibility of data science throughout organization. How can you trust what data says if it only says it once, and when you ask it again it gives you a different answer?

> How can you trust what data says if it only says it once, and when you ask it again it gives you a different answer?

Once I had to prepare a report on an A/B test we ran in *Candy Crush*. I got in touch with a fellow data scientist from another office and suggested that we also do a "meta A/B test." Each of us would independently prepare a report—using the same data—and then compare our figures, e.g., uplift in players' engagement and spend.

The results of this meta A/B test were a rude awakening. The numbers we would hypothetically report to a wider audience without a second thought were nowhere near "close enough."

The discrepancy was not result of an error, but of differences in our approach to measuring the impact on business metrics. It was not even clear which approach was right. We could take two sets of noticeably different numbers to decision-makers and tell them to pick whichever they liked more.

So much for objective and data-driven.

Shareable

As we discussed in Part I, the end goal of data science is to change opinions. This, obviously, requires that the end result of a data analysis reach people whose opinion matters. It also matters how and when it does so.

Let's imagine a data scientist tasked with producing a monthly sales report for the company leadership. He or she can deliver the report in several different ways:

- Email the report.

    Job done. No-one can say that the report has not been delivered. It is also shareable—in the sense that a person who has received it can forward it to someone else. However, when it comes to *discovering* this information in future, this approach relies on the recipient's proficiency in managing their inbox and files. In practice, most people will struggle to find the report a few weeks down the road.

- Upload the report to centralized storage (shared folder, corporate portal, knowledge base, etc.)

    With all monthly reports in one location, decision-makers will have a much easier time discovering and exploring them. A bookmark in their browser will be enough for them to be able to look up any past report in a few clicks.

- Create an online report that displays sales figures for any chosen month.

    This may seem like a small step from the previous approach, but by removing the dependency on external software (which can make a big difference on a mobile device) and saving the user another click or two, the data scientist has further lowered the barrier between the data and its consumer.

Shareability creates a virtuous cycle: provided the information is useful, as it becomes easier to discover and explore there will be demand for more, which will make it easier to invest in data science.

***

Together, simplicity, reproducibility, and shareability create a solid foundation for data science that serves people.

glossary

User interface (UI) is the space of interaction between a piece of software and its operator.

works cited

"People Systematically Overlook Subtractive Changes" / Gabrielle S. Adams, Benjamin A. Converse, Andrew H. Hales et al. / 2021 *Nature* 592: 258–261.

The Visual Display of Quantitative Data / Edward Tufte / 1983 Graphics Press.

quality assurance

Quality assurance (QA) is a standard practice in many fields. Software development is a good example, with quite a few data scientists coming over from that industry.

I do not think I have ever overheard software developers discussing whether or not it makes sense to have a QA process, in addition to writing code itself. The assumption appears to be that if code is written it must be tested.

Furthermore, while software developers are encouraged to at least sanity check their code, the common practice is to have dedicated QA people, who do not write product code themselves and focus on testing code written by software developers. These are two fundamentally distinct activities that require different mindsets. A developer normally operates with the mindset of "How to make this work?," whereas a QA person—"How to break this?"

Data analysis is similar to software development in the sense that the person doing it is focused on working their way to an answer, or a pretty looking report, or a dashboard that works at all. They may not be equally focused on making sure that the answer is correct, the report—error-free, and the dashboard—easy to understand. Speaking from personal experience, once I have been working on something for a couple of days, I stop really seeing the numbers. They become background noise my brain filters out. On more than one occasion, I would change something and not notice that a significant chunk of my report or dashboard has disappeared altogether. Luckily, this kind of mistake would usually be pointed out by someone who actually needed that chunk. (If it was not, then perhaps no-one actually needed it.)

DOI: 10.1201/9781003057420-7

In Chapter 2, we saw that data science may need QA even more so than software development, in the sense that the end-user of a piece of software is more likely to notice a problem with it than the end-user of a piece of data analysis. Still, I am yet to see a structured and thorough data science QA process, even though I have been privileged to work in several different organizations, with varying levels of data maturity and the size and structure of the data science team.

It seems logical to first discuss why QA in data science does not get as much attention as it should. We will then proceed to talking in more detail about what and how should be QA'ed.

See if you can find any typos in this chapter.

what makes QA difficult?

It is relatively easy to demonstrate the importance of a vigorous QA process for data science: take any complex data analysis that has not been double- and triple-checked, and you have a good chance of discovering if not an outright error then, at least, a contentious choice. Or try and reproduce someone else's numbers and plots without re-using their code. It will not take long until you find something that (would) have had serious consequences.

Then why is not QA a prominent subject in the domain of data science? From personal experience and conversations with other data people, I have identified the following challenges when it comes to setting up a QA process in a data science team:

Individual Mindset

The thought that you may have made an error is an unpleasant one. The degree to which it is unpleasant mainly depends on three factors:

- How much effort it would take to correct the error.
- How much effort you have already put into the task would have been wasted (sunk cost fallacy).
- How stupid you would look if someone knew.

It is one problem if you do realize that you may have made an error, but you simply refuse to go back and check. This would indicate that you do not actually care about your results being correct. Or you do not care enough. A scrupulous QA process could help in this case, but it would only cure the symptoms, not the root cause. If you ever find yourself doing data science (or any kind of science, for that matter) and not making being correct your top priority, then you should stop immediately and seek help.

It is a different problem, and a more insidious one, if you mentally shirk away from the very thought that your analysis may be wrong. This happens on the subconscious level, and therefore requires a great deal of concentration and self-discipline to even notice, let alone prevent.

In his *Twelve Virtues of Rationality*,[1] Eliezer Yudkowsky writes: "Do not flinch from experiences that might destroy your beliefs. The thought you cannot think controls you more than thoughts you speak aloud."

In this case, you must learn to not flinch from any suspicion that might destroy your belief in your analysis being correct, and your work being flawless. You are a scientist, and your analysis is your theory. As a good scientist, you should welcome any opportunity to pitch your theory against criticism and counterarguments. If your theory is valid this kind of opposition will only make it stronger. If not, it will collapse, and you should be okay with it.

That said, you can help yourself by minimizing the factors that contribute to the unpleasantness of realizing you might have made a mistake.

Minimize the effort it would take to correct an error. For example, one fundamental problem with doing data science in a spreadsheet is that it entangles data, calculations, and visualizations. If you notice an error in the data, it is likely to have a trickle-down effect: you may have to painstakingly update every pivot table and every plot. Whereas if you are using a programming language (and using it correctly) the error will be contained within its segment, and you will only need to re-run the script once you have corrected the mistake.

Minimize the effort that would have been wasted. Similarly, try and make your code as general and modular as possible. The less new and task-specific code you write, the less you will have to throw away should you realize it was a wrong approach. You want to be "smart lazy" and get results with the least effort possible. Other people only care about the results, and your hard work does not impart any extra value. Your hard work only increases your sunk cost and makes it more difficult for you to go back to the drawing board.

> Other people only care about the results, and your hard work does not impart any extra value.

Minimize perceived reputation damage. Obviously, the best approach is to find and correct your mistakes before anyone else has a chance to discover them for you, whether it is an internal reviewer or an end-user. This is an integral process of doing data science, and ideally you would want to spend enough time verifying your assumptions, logic, and implementation. In reality, it is often difficult to find faults in your work past a certain point, as you develop a certain kind of blindness. A fresh pair of eyes (connected to a well-functioning brain) will see things in a different light, and almost always find things you long before stopped noticing.

Whether you are submitting your work for a review or delivering it to the end-user, you can take pre-emptive measures by adding a footnote: "These are preliminary results. Do not share them broadly while I am double-checking everything. Let me know if anything looks off to you." At least, when a silly mistake is inevitably discovered, you will be able to hold your hands up and say, "I told you it was just a draft."

Ultimately, the ability to accept one's mistakes with grace is a skill worth mastering. Or so I am told.

Team Culture

It is a normal practice to have dedicated software testers doing QA of software developers' work. While something similar can be done by non-data people with respect to data science—sanity check of the results—any thorough QA process involves other data scientists.

This may vary from culture to culture, but generally people are reluctant to verify others' work and point out mistakes. It is a social challenge to criticize a team-mate's work—no matter how constructively—and not come across as a bit of a knob. Simply telling data scientists to start doing QA for each other may fall short, as they will find it tempting to report that the other person has done an excellent job, and that they have got nothing but, perhaps, a minor suggestion or two. This attitude will damage the initiative both directly, in that serious errors will go undiscovered, and indirectly, in that it will distort the meta feedback loop by creating the impression that your QA process adds little value.

People are complicated, and there is no silver bullet, but there a few things that may help you get started:

Let it come from within. I have never met a data science manager who understood the necessity of a QA process well enough to make it an explicit part of the process (one of the reasons this book has been written), so the initiative will probably have to come from data scientists themselves anyway. Nonetheless, it is important to remember that the quality of QA is very sensitive to the goodwill of the person doing it. You can hardly expect a conscientious effort from someone if you shoved a vague and unwelcome task down their throat.

Start small. It may be easier to start with a single, particularly important project. Is someone working on a report for the board of directors? Or an A/B test that is going to decide whether or a not a game will be launched? Or a predictive model that will identify potential targets in the next transfer window? It will only look sensible to assign a second data scientist to double-check the results.

Set an example. Whether they realize it or not, people are protective of their status in the social hierarchy, in this case, the hierarchy at the workplace. Admitting our mistakes or, more generally, that we can learn from someone may present a danger to our status. The more secure we feel about our status, the easier it is to learn from others.

As a new hire or a junior data scientist, you will feel much more comfortable about exposing your work to criticism if you have seen your senior colleagues do that and their mistakes exposed without any reputational damage. This is a clear signal that being wrong does not necessarily ruin your social standing, and that the flawlessness of your work is not strongly coupled with your public image.

Us vs them. If the organization is blessed with multiple data science teams, especially in different locations, you can harness the inevitable rivalry between them. Instead of feeling bad about destroying a team-mate's analysis, people can get competitive and eager to prove that their team is better. Done in a healthy way, this may have a positive side-effect of the increased knowledge exchange and collaboration between the teams.

Resources

When you decide to add QA to your data science activities, you may run into the problem of everyone already working at 100% of their capacity, or close enough. Or at least saying that is the case.

First of all, the problem must be acknowledged. QA is done for a good reason, but it does come at a cost. You cannot simply ask people to start doing more, everything else staying as it is.

One can find a lot of advice on how to carve out time for "hackathons," "hack days," or even "hack weeks," to give data scientists an opportunity to learn and explore, but I have not seen anything along the same lines for QA.

The main difference between setting aside time for "hacking" and QA is that the former is usually not connected to an existing project, whereas the latter definitely is. A team I was part of once tried to have "QA Tuesday," but it did not work very well. In hindsight, it was clear that timing is important when it comes to QA. You do it when a project is finished, not on Tuesday.

If you are using a task management system (Basecamp, Trello, JIRA, a board with sticky notes), you may want to create a separate QA task for every project that needs to be QA'ed. This will explicitly allocate someone's time to do the review, and equate checking someone else's work with doing one's own, both in terms of recognition and accountability.

When a new task is created and assigned to a data scientist, it is most helpful to assign the respective QA task at the same time. It gives the second data scientist a chance to participate in a two-person project planning meeting, serve as a rubber duck,[2] and be much more informed about the ins and outs of the analysis when it is time to verify its results.

Also, a situation in which one person explains their thinking and another tries to understand it is an ideal learning opportunity. And these may be scarce when each data scientist works in solitude.

what is there to QA?

Let's imagine you and your team have addressed the challenges outlined above. Everyone is on board. A piece of data analysis has just been completed, and you have allocated time to give it a proper QA treatment. How exactly do you go about it?

Consider a simple scenario:

- The analysis is based on a set of data managed by someone else, e.g., a data warehouse team.
- A data scientist wrote some code (SQL, R, Python, etc.) that produces some results (numbers and plots).
- The numbers and plots will be presented to "decision-makers" once the analysis has passed QA.

At first glance, it would appear that we are dealing with three components:

Data in, code does something, results out. Simples.
But let's take a closer look at each box.

Data

As we saw in Chapter 1, the very process of data collection can be complex and require a lot of decisions to be made before the data is ready to be used by a data scientist. It is a good practice to have a separate QA process for it. In a large data-driven organization, with a dedicated data engineer or a whole data warehouse team, this is likely to fall into their lap. Without a data engineer, the data scientists will have to QA data themselves. This will be yet another task they have to allocate resources for, but there will be a nice side-effect of them being intimately familiar with the data.

When the data is collected and processed automatically, the QA process around it is essentially the same as that for software development. After all, it is software that "creates" data. Manual data collection presents a different set of challenges. Either way, making sure the data is reliable should be external to data analysis.

In the ideal world, all data available to data scientists would have been validated and verified by a separate team of qualified data engineers, and some organizations do aspire to this ideal.

Ultimately, it is a spectrum:

No data engineers.	A team of data engineers.
A bunch of spreadsheets.	Data is collected automatically.
Manual data entry.	All data goes through rigorous QA.

←————————————————————————————————————→

Data scientist should perform complete data QA. A quick sanity check should suffice.

Whether or not you are a football fan, you might be interested to know that all English Premier League stadiums have several special video cameras installed along the perimeter. During a game, these cameras track positions of the football players and the ball. The tracking data can be used to analyze tactical and physical performance of the teams and individual players.

When a Premier League team travels to a stadium lacking this setup (e.g., a cup tie against a low-tier club or European competition), the data provider may send a couple of people who collect tracking data using portable equipment.

When Arsenal played away at Napoli in the Europa League 2018/19, the tracking data was unusually "jittery." The total distance each player covered was not significantly affected, but speed (first derivative of distance) was. As for acceleration and deceleration (second derivatives), they were off the scale.

When modelling players' physical output, that game had to be removed from the data set, otherwise the inflated values would skew season averages.

Code

This little box in the diagram packs a lot.

First, we should remember that data is not reality, but a mere reflection of it. As we saw in Chapter 1 even "raw" data is a result of some data collection process. Whatever the relationship between reality and the data, it needs to be understood. And whenever something needs to be understood, there is a risk of it being understood incorrectly.

For example, I may be looking at a footballer's training load and notice a gap of a week or two with no load at all. I may assume the player was injured and I will be wrong—he was away with his national team and did train. It is just that we did not get any data from the national team. There is nothing wrong with the data we have. The problem is that I assumed the data we have is a complete reflection of the reality in the context of players' training load. It is not the data that needed to be verified, but my assumptions.

For a more subtle example, I may assume that training session date + player name is a unique combination that identifies a player's training session. And I would be wrong again: it is not unusual to have two training sessions on the same day during pre-season.

Once we have established, explicitly or implicitly, our assumptions about the data, we need to design a high-level approach to how we are going to turn data into results. A simple research question may have only one viable approach, for example:

Question: How many transactions did we process in 2020?

Approach: Count the number of rows in the table transactions where column date has a value that starts with "2020-."

A more complicated question will force you to explore a multitude of possible ways to answer it:

Question: How much does the mobile game we just released "cannibalize" on the existing games, i.e., draws away from their user base?

Approach: Have a few lengthy discussions before even getting started.

An experienced data scientist is likely to seek a peer review of their chosen approach before they write a single line of code:

[...] the main motivation for data scientists to get peer review of the research phase of their projects is to prevent them from choosing the wrong approach or direction in this early phase of the project. These errors — referred to as approach failures in the DS workflow — are very costly to make, and they impede the project for the rest of its lifecycle.

Only now, having made their assumptions and chosen their approach, can the data scientist start the magical process of turning data into results.

You may have heard that data "wrangling" or "cleaning" takes up to 80% or 90% of a data scientist's time. From what I can tell based on my own experience, this is not a massive exaggeration.

"The reason that data wrangling is so difficult is that data is more than text and numbers."[3] Unless you are doing data science in the ideal world of an online course where you are given a carefully groomed or even artificially created data set, you will have to deal with any of the following problems:

- Missing values, when a piece of data is simply not there.
- Inconsistent format, e.g., dates changing from "01/03/04" to "May 1, 2004" halfway through the data set.
- Inconsistent nomenclature, e.g., football player names which can come with or without initials, or with special characters ("Mesut Özil" or "M. Ozil").
- Lack of context, e.g., when you can see values, but you are uncertain what they stand for. You may need "meta data" that describes the relationship between values and real world.

Things get even more complicated when you have to merge multiple data sets, each with its unique issues.

For many data science tasks, having successfully wrangled the data means getting very close to completing the task. To answer a simple business query, you may only need to count table rows or total up values in a column. But even in the case of machine learning, it is entirely possible that, with a clean data set at your disposal, all you need to do is write a single line of code to train your predictive model and another line to evaluate the model's accuracy. And whatever the advancements in the field of machine learning, and no matter how deep your knowledge of algorithms, the importance of data wrangling shall not budge.

Let's amend the diagram so that it reflects everything that goes on inside "Code":

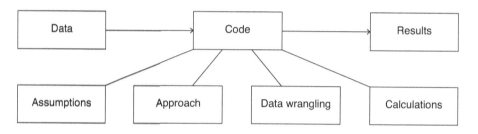

Results

Now it is time to remember that the actual output of data science is a change in someone's opinion. Not numbers, plots or dashboards, but the difference between what someone thought before looking at them and what they think after.

The data can be perfect, the data scientist's assumptions correct, the results on the mark, but none of it will matter if the end-user of the analysis misunderstands it. Conveying results to the audience is a step as important as anything that precedes it.

This is the most challenging part of the data science process. You cannot "make" someone correctly interpret the results of an analysis, or a plot, or a dashboard. There is a lot you can do to help them, to make it easier, to lead a horse to water, so to speak, but ultimately it depends on the willingness of the recipient if they are going to take the message in.

Ironically, a data scientist enters this last phase when they feel the job has been done. They have crunched the numbers, made beautiful plots, put together a slick presentation. What else are they supposed to do, except perhaps send out an email? Haven't they done enough? Don't they deserve a break, a cup of tea and a biscuit?

They do. But the work is not done yet. Just like creating product does not make a business successful and is only a prerequisite to advertising and selling, completing a data science product is only a prerequisite to communicating it and changing people's opinions.

Let's amend the diagram once more:

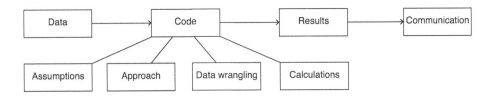

Now, what do we do with this?

how to QA all this?

When thinking about QA, it makes sense to start at the right end of the diagram:

Communication

This is arguably the most important and at the same time the vaguest area of the process. "Data translator" may be the next sexiest job of the 21st century.[4] At the moment, however, most companies have to make do with the same data scientist who has made the thing to be communicated.

The most important factor in communication of data science results is consistency. The less is left open to interpretation, the less risk of misinterpretation.

Consistency is a spectrum, and we can look at a few distinct levels:

- **No structure at all**: Every data scientist reports results as they see fit. This is obviously not ideal and leaves a lot of room for interpretation and personal biases.
- **Shared vocabulary**: Data scientists and everyone else have the same idea of what, for example, "DAU" or "conversion rate" are. This is the bare minimum required for effectively communicating data science results. Many organizations can be found at this level.

When I worked with mobile games, two important business metrics were "second day retention" and "seventh day retention."

Second day retention was the percentage of players who were active on the next day after installing the game. For example, if 100 people installed the game on Monday, and 50 of them were active on Tuesday, then second day retention was 50%.

Seventh day retention was the percentage of players who were active one week later—on the same day of the week—after installing the game. The problem with this metric was that, technically, it should have been named "8th day retention": if you installed the game on Monday, and it was day 1, then Monday next week was day 8.

And yes, it did happen that sometimes data scientists and business analysts were using different calculations even for this seemingly simple metric.

- **Templates**: A template serves multiple purposes:
  - Informs the data scientist as to what information is expected.
  - Informs the audience as to what information they should expect. (Imagine a freshly hired game producer, who is still learning the ropes. They may not be immediately aware of what business metrics their game is going to be judged by.)
  - Allows a side-by-side comparison.

For example, let's imagine data scientists reporting the results of the launch of two mobile games.

- **Game X**: We have seen 3.6 million installs after the first 10 days. Of the players who installed the game within the first 3 days, 36% were active in the last 2 days, which shows good retention. 5% have converted into paying users, which is in line with our expectations...
- **Game Y**: We have had 1.5 million installs on iOS and another 1.4 on Android in the first week. 2nd day retention is 48% and 45%, respectively. Total gross bookings are at $465,000...

If you were to compare Game X and Game Y side by side, you would probably find it difficult, if not outright impossible, the way the data had been presented to you. It would be much easier if games' KPI's were to be recorded using a template:

7 Days Since Launch	Game X	Game Y
Installs (total, million)	**2.7**	**2.9**
iOS		1.5
Android		1.4
2nd day retention	**38%**	**47%**
iOS		48%
Android		45%
Overall conversion rate	**5%**	
iOS		
Android		
Gross bookings		**$465,000**
iOS		
Android		

Bold values represent the totals (across iOS and Android platforms)

Where you have got data for both games, the comparison is straightforward. Wherever data is missing, you are immediately aware of it and can decide what to do about it.

- **Automated reporting.**

    Everything that is reported is reported via automatically generated reports, dashboards, etc. For example, in a mature A/B test framework, the results of every A/B test will be communicated on the same dashboard. All the numbers will be displayed just the way they are displayed for any other A/B test. All the plots will look just the way they look for any other A/B test. The only thing that changes is the actual lines, or bars, or colors corresponding to the results. The same set of KPI's, the same user categories, the same splits (by platform, browser, etc.)—the ultimate "apples to apples."

    Consistency is just one of the benefits of automation. We will talk more about automation in Chapter 6.

* * *

Communication of the results cannot be verified unless there is a two-way discussion. It is not enough for the data scientist to present their work to the respective audience. It is not enough to allow some time for Q&A. When people have misunderstood something, they do not know it. Nor do they always realize when they have not understood something completely. And even when they do, people do not like to look stupid, and asking a simple question when everyone else in the meeting-room is nodding along feels like a sure way to look stupid.

Comprehension is not practically "QA-able" in the same sense as the preceding steps. While you can ask someone to verify the data you used, the assumptions you made, your code and the results it produced, it would make little sense to suggest that they also check whether or not your audience received your message as it was intended.

In most situations, even the data scientist delivering the results cannot conduct a comprehension check. More often than not, they are presenting to "important" people, and it is not done to look at an important person and ask, "Can you repeat what I have just explained in your own words?"

Some things to try:

- Present to a smaller group, even if it means multiple presentations to several groups. It will make it easier for people to come out with questions.

- Send out key results via email or similar, so that people can peruse them privately. Should they have follow-up questions, they will be able to choose between "Reply" and "Reply All." (This assumes that people open and read emails from a data scientist, which is not a given.)

- If at all possible, talk to key decision-makers face-to-face.

Having said all this, you still need to verify the results you are going to communicate.

Results

Results is the ultimate target for QA. In many situations, it makes sense to verify some of the results and stop there. If you can reliably verify one number or one plot, then you can extrapolate the conclusion, if the analysis is right or wrong, to all other numbers or plots that were created using the same approach.

The catch is that to reliably verify the results of a piece of data science, you have to reproduce it independently, which potentially doubles the amount of work. However, you can save time and effort by focusing your attention on a subset of the results:

- just one metric;
- just one group, segment or cohort of users;
- just one time period instead of the entire timeline...

If the original analysis took 5 days to be done, and you can only allocate 1 day for QA, try and reproduce the key 20% of the results. If the discrepancy between the original results and those reproduced as part of the QA process is within the acceptable margin—excellent, a job well done! Otherwise, the two parties have to put their heads together and figure out why they arrive at different conclusions.

For example, let's say the original analysis resulted in a set of measurements shown on this bar plot:

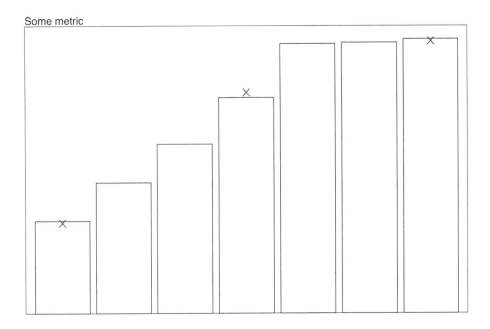

To save time on QA, we can decide to independently reproduce only three measurements, in the middle and at the extremes, shown as crosses.

While the reproduced values do not match the original results exactly, the discrepancy is small relative to the observed range. In most business settings, this would be "close enough" to put a stamp of approval on the analysis.

Occasionally, an analysis does have to be reproduced in its entirety, and it is an excellent opportunity to appreciate all the decisions that went into it, often without much deliberation.

I once had to help a software developer reproduce one of my reports as part of a reporting platform his was building. My report was written in R and the developer was using a different programming language, so he could not simply copy and paste my code.

It took us a relatively short back-and-forth (3–4 emails each way) to go through the basics of the report—what I believed to be a set of trivial data transformations: filter, add up, multiply and divide. "Does not get much simpler," I thought.

It turned out it was simple only because I had already done it. Once the developer reproduced the calculations, he had numbers and they were different from mine. It took us another 5–6 rounds of correspondence, each of them getting rid of a potential source of the discrepancy, to make the numbers match.

It usually pays off to do a "sanity check" of the results before trying to reproduce them.

It is often the case that data analysis produces results that can be verified, at least approximately, using common sense and/or alternative data sources.

For example, if I have created a detailed football match report with various metrics and dimensions, I can check if total distance covered by the team is (1) plausible and (2) comparable to that reported on sports websites. If there is a significant discrepancy, I will have a good reason to suspect that I have made a mistake.

For another example, let's say you have been running an A/B test on your entire user base, with two groups: experimental and control, 50% of users each. The analysis shows a 20% uplift in revenue per user in the experimental group relative to the control group. However, when you look at the revenue report, you do not see a 10% uptick you would expect to see if that were true. Without looking anywhere else, you have already got a strong case for redoing the analysis.

This kind of sanity check can be performed by a non-data person, too. So, even if there are no data scientists available to do "proper" QA, asking a businessperson to eyeball the results can be an efficient way of taking QA from zero to an acOceptable level. It is not so much about resources as it is about the attitude of everyone involved.

> It is not so much about resources as it is about the attitude of everyone involved.

Should you be satisfied with independently reproduced results, you can call it a day and have a great deal more of faith in the analysis. This does happen sometimes. Otherwise you should not be surprised if you find a significant discrepancy. This raises an awkward question: "Who is wrong?" Or, more pessimistically, "Is either of us right?" It is time to roll up the sleeves and go through the code to identify where the discrepancy comes from.

Code

I have seen it too many times that people equate data science QA with code review. I would show them my analysis or dashboard asking to test it, and they would review the code and nothing else. They might ask a question or two, or suggest how this or that could be implemented differently, but if I was honest with myself I would know that this review hardly made me more confident in my work.

Code review does not work as QA for data analysis.

If you look at software development, the purpose of code review is not to find errors. Finding errors is the job of software testers, whereas code review is there to enforce best practices and facilitate knowledge exchange. Code review in

> Code review does not work as QA for data analysis.

data analytics can serve similar purposes, but it will hardly help you discover errors, unless they are blatantly obvious, in which case the reviewer is more of a tutor.

> I used to work with a data scientist who liked to compose a deeply nested SQL query, a cacophony of SELECT and JOIN statements, and then email it to me with a question, "Do you think this will work?"
>
> I had not yet learnt how to say no, so I would sigh, take the query, and meticulously break it into CTE's. Then, I would do a sanity check on each of them and fuse them one by one—again, validating the output at every step. Instinctively, I knew there was no easier way to make sure a complex query did what we expected.

QA creates a feedback loop for data science projects. You also need a feedback loop for the QA process itself. This is especially important if you are just beginning to implement it. In addition to asking the standard questions—what works, what does not, and how it can be improved—it is useful to keep track of which projects went through QA, whether or not any problems were found, and how it affected the project in question.

Until QA process has become an integral part of the data science team culture, people will be tempted to doubt that its benefits are worth the time and effort. Whether it is true or not, just like data science helps people base their decisions on hard facts rather than their perception, collecting data about your QA process with help evaluate its impact objectively.

Implemented well, QA process will address data issues, your understanding of the data, how you analyze it and how the results are interpreted by the target audience.

glossary

Common table expression (CTE) is a temporary result set used in the SQL code to simplify complex joins and subqueries.
Sunk cost fallacy is a tendency to continue an endeavor once an investment has been made. "Throwing good money after bad."

works cited

The Visual Display of Quantitative Data / Edward Tufte / 1983 Graphics Press.

notes

1 http://yudkowsky.net/rational/virtues.

2 In *The Pragmatic Programmer* (1999), a programmer would carry around a rubber duck and debug their code by forcing themselves to explain it, line-by-line, to the duck.

3 "Wrangling Unruly Data: The Bane of Every Data Science Team," Carl Howe. https://blog.rstudio.com/2020/05/05/wrangling-unruly-data/.

4 https://hbr.org/2018/02/you-dont-have-to-be-a-data-scientist-to-fill-this-must-have-analytics-role.

automation

I rarely speak at conferences, averaging about one a year. When I do, I speak about something that feels important to me. In 2016, I gave a talk titled "Why You Mustn't Listen to a Data Scientist" (Gaming Analytics Summit, March 3–4, 2016, London). Which I still consider the peak of my career as a conference speaker. It is closely followed by the presentation I gave a year later: "Data Science without a Data Scientist," which was about automation. I had recently started building data pipelines and automated reports and was full of enthusiasm. And for a good reason.

Science and technology are the closest thing to magic we have got. Arguably, it is better than magic we usually see in books and movies. It is getting more powerful at an exponential rate, and its benefits are felt by more people, regardless of how much science and technology they know themselves.

Automation plays a big role in the magic of science and technology. A process that does not require human input can be improved beyond human capabilities in terms of speed, quality and reliability. And, very importantly, automation frees people up to do something more interesting.

As this book is about data science, we will have to dispense with the wonders of engineering in the world of steam engines and conveyor belts, and focus on what automation can do in the realm of databases, spreadsheets and pie charts.

Automation in data analysis generally boils down to writing software that replaces human operator in moving data around, transforming it into meaningful numbers and data visualizations, and delivering human-friendly outputs to stakeholders, e.g., via email or an online dashboard.

DOI: 10.1201/9781003057420-8

It is not always part of a data scientist's job to write software code. Oftentimes, this duty crawls over a fuzzy line and drops into the lap of a data or software engineer. In the area of machine learning, there is usually a clearer divide between a data scientist (research, exploratory analysis, building a model) and an ML engineer (putting models into "production"—incorporating them into a customer-facing product). That said, while the ability to write code does not define a data scientist, it does act as a value multiplier. Whether a data scientist is working alone or in a team, they can do so much more if they have got programming experience and are comfortable with variables and operators, conditional logic and loops, functions and libraries.

This is a big topic, and as with any big topic, the best way to get the hang of it is to start with a story.

> While the ability to write code does not define a data scientist, it does act as a value multiplier.

the automation story

My personal journey from manual labor, as much as this term can be applied to data science, to a "lights-out"[1] data analysis took place soon after I joined King. The company already had a culture of running A/B tests to make decisions about game design. I and other data scientists had to analyze the data and present findings to game development teams. In 2–3 years, we moved through a few distinct phases of how we would do it.

Phase 1: "Manual" Data Science

Early on, I had to familiarize myself with the data available in the company databases and ask senior colleagues when something was unclear. I would run a few SQL queries to fetch data, such as player assignment to test groups and their activity in the game, then import it in a spreadsheet, so that I could have my fun with it.

I would do some exploratory analysis to verify my assumptions (e.g., that players are split evenly between test groups), then calculate business metrics (retention rate, conversion rate, etc.) for each test group. Next step would be turning numbers into plots with multi-colored lines and helpful annotations.

Finally, I would create a stack of slides, in which the plots were accompanied by the description of the A/B test setup, conclusions derived from the results, potential caveats, and suggestions for future research.

This was bread-and-butter of data-driven business intelligence. Such a hands-on approach had its pros and cons:

Pros:	Cons:
• I was forced to explore and learn about the company data with my own eyes (Chapter 1: Why It Is Important to Understand Your Data). • Working with data in a spreadsheet, I had to perform each operation manually, which ensured that I knew exactly what was happening ("Column A is divided by column B..."). • I would receive direct feedback in response to my presentation. I would learn what different stakeholders wanted, and how they saw and reasoned about numbers and data visualizations.	• The process was time-consuming. It could take a few days to analyze a single A/B test. • Any change (adding a metric or redesigning a plot) would take considerable time and effort. • Analysis would be hard to reproduce. If I wanted to share my method with someone, I would have to sit them down and show them what I did in the spreadsheet. • Every manual operation introduced risk of a human error. Clicking on the wrong column or making a typo in a formula could ruin the entire analysis (Chapter 2: Domino of mistakes). • Results would be a presentation file, normally shared via email. If a colleague had recently joined and/or had to look up an old report, they would have to go on a quest.

Phase 2: Templates

Having analyzed a few A/B tests using the "manual" approach, I have developed a comprehensive set of SQL queries that would produce all the numbers I needed for my report. I knew what metrics the business stakeholders might be interested in, and I had them all covered.

When I noticed that I was using essentially the same SQL code, only changing the name of the A/B test and dates when it ran, I created a template that made it explicit: enter the parameters at the top, run the entire thing, the output is saved into a CSV file, ready to be imported in a spreadsheet. The spreadsheet itself would also be a template: for a new analysis, I would only replace the data and then simply update calculations and plots downstream. It would not be as flexible as I would have liked it. For example, if the new A/B test had a different number of test groups I would still have to make adjustments, but it was still miles better than doing everything from scratch.

"A journey of a thousand miles begins with a single step." As far as automation goes, this was child's play, but it highlighted a few benefits of moving away from doing things by hand:

- It saved time.
- It reduced opportunities for making a mistake.
- It ensured consistency in calculations of business metrics.

Phase 3: Script

As a fledging data scientist, I had a difficulty letting go of doing things by hand. A modern data scientist is generally expected to know one or both of the most popular programming languages for data analysis: R and Python. It was the former that was primarily used by my more experienced colleagues. While I had done programming outside data analysis, I nonetheless found the learning curve a bit of a challenge.

Wrangling and plotting data in a spreadsheet is time-consuming and error prone. A lot of pointing and clicking is often required, and sometimes you have to do it all over again, as changes manually made to one spreadsheet or chart will not be automatically replicated elsewhere. Yet these shortcomings are easy to ignore until you have learned a better way. And to learn the better way you need motivation that comes from feeling the shortcomings. Catch-22.

RStudio, the IDE most used for R programming, is a great tool for exploring and working with data, but it still takes some getting used to when switching over from a spreadsheet, where all the data is literally in front of you. There are also powerful libraries for data wrangling and visualization (e.g., "dplyr" and "ggplot2"), but they are a far cry from pivot tables and charts. Writing code is so much less visceral than pointing, clicking and dragging.

In hindsight, while it is understandable why it took me a while to warm up to doing data analysis and visualization by writing code, I wish I had done gone over more quickly. It is a recurring lesson: if you know that you are going to have to learn a new time-saving tool *eventually*, better do it sooner. It will take the same effort, but you will start reaping the rewards earlier.

Slowly but surely, I reproduced everything I used to do in spreadsheets in R code. Very quickly, I was able to feel the benefits of automation magic. Before, if I wanted to change, for example, the color or thickness of my line charts, I had to meticulously go through them one by one. Now I only had to change one parameter in my code, re-run it and, lo and behold, all the plots would be updated, regardless of how many I had.

> If you know that you are going to have to learn a new time-saving tool eventually, better do it sooner. It will take the same effort, but you will start reaping the rewards earlier.

It was a big step up from using an SQL template and it brought new, massive benefits:

- It saved even more time.
- It made it much easier to change calculations and visualizations—I could try things that I would not try before, as it would not have been worth the effort.

- It further reduced opportunities for mistakes.

   When you point and click, drag and drop, copy and paste hundreds of times you are bound to miss every now and again without noticing.

- It allowed me to share my code.

   When you share a spreadsheet, it does not include your actions, and it may take the other person a lot of investigating and guessing to figure out where the numbers come from and how they are connected to each other. Reading someone else's code is not always easy, but it is a surmountable task compared to understanding an equally complex spreadsheet.

- In addition to calculations, it also ensured consistency in presentation.

   All plots would be created by running the same code instead of crafted manually for every presentation.

Phase 4: Full Automation

The company was growing, and so were the data science team and the number of A/B tests running at any given moment. Grassroots efforts to standardize and automate the analysis of A/B tests morphed into a cross-team project that culminated in the ultimate solution: a centralized, fully automated online dashboard.

Most A/B tests did not require the involvement of a data scientist at all now. A business stakeholder would simply open the dashboard in their Internet browser, select the A/B test they were interested in, and see its daily and cumulative numbers and plots.

It was automation magic at its finest:

- Data scientists did not have to spend their time on mundane analysis anymore and could focus on more challenging and interesting projects. They could still be asked to do a "deep dive" into a specific A/B test to uncover the finer details of player behavior, but anything repetitive had been moved to the dashboard.

- It ensured the ultimate consistency, as every single A/B test was analyzed and reported on by the same software.

- It simplified quality assurance. All QA efforts would be focused on a single codebase. When you have got one script that calculates a business metric across dozens, perhaps hundreds of A/B tests, it is easy to convince people that it is important to verify that it is doing what is expected.

- It presented results whenever they were needed. Instead of waiting for a stack of slides from a data scientist, anyone could go the webpage and get the most up-to-date outputs.

- It was maximally shareable. As long as people had the link, all past and future reports had effectively been shared with them. There were no presentations to be sent over email. It did not matter how long ago an A/B test report had been run— you could look it up just as easily as if it happened yesterday.

underappreciated benefits

The story above nicely demonstrates the various benefits of automation, but some of them are worth taking a closer look at, as they often go underappreciated.

Always Moving Forward

By its nature, automation lets people free themselves of repetitive tasks that do not require human creativity and ingenuity. Data science is not a trade that benefits from polishing a narrow skill. Once you have analyzed three or four A/B tests and nailed down the final product (a set of numbers and plots that go into your report), there is little benefit in practicing it for 10,000 hours.[2]

There are disciplines—sports, dance, playing a musical instrument— in which patience and diligence in doing the same thing over and over again are commendable qualities for a practitioner. It is exactly the opposite for a data scientist: if you see one who is comfortable performing the same tasks day in day out, they are probably in the wrong job.

One of the most inspiring data people I have been fortunate to work with used to say, "If a data scientist does the same thing three times, they should be fired."

That was a bit of an exaggeration, but only a bit.

A data scientist who does not look for new challenges (and that requires solving existing challenges for good) will soon plateau, while one who keeps learning, conquering and moving on will be ever more useful and impactful.

> If a data scientist does the same thing three times, they should be fired.

A good data scientist does not mind boring, mundane and repetitive tasks, but understands what and why needs to be done, builds tools to have it done automatically, and moves on to new challenges.

Better Quality Assurance

Another benefit of automation that can be easily overlooked is that it facilitates quality assurance.

First, manual repetitive tasks, especially those with a lot of moving parts, are the perfect breeding ground for errors and mistakes. A human performing them can get distracted or grow tired. Mis-clicks and typos ensue. A piece of software has no such weaknesses.

> A good data scientist does not mind boring, mundane and repetitive tasks, but understands what and why needs to be done, builds tools to have it done automatically, and moves on to new challenges.

Second, when you write code to automate a task, that code only needs to be verified once. As long as the task and environment stay the same, once you have made sure that the code does what it is supposed to do, there is no reason to worry that it will lose its ways later on. (It can be argued that a piece of code may have worked flawlessly with the inputs used in verification but can malfunction given an unusual input, a so-called "edge case." This is why automation can be premature, and we are going to talk about it in a minute.)

Another aspect of automation that is beneficial from QA's point of view is that, when something goes wrong in an automated process, it usually goes wrong in an obvious manner: at some point the process breaks down, and an error message or warning is produced. While this fragility may be frustrating, it forces the person in charge to investigate what has happened and make sure it does not happen again. People are more flexible than software and more capable of overlooking a problem.

> People are more flexible than software and more capable of overlooking a problem.

Fast Delivery

In the world of data, people often say "big", but very rarely "fresh". In the context of changing opinions and making decisions, data always has a shelf life. Sometimes, a rather short shelf life. When it is a race against the clock, automation may be not just a better way to perform a task, but the *only* way. Let's look at an example from the trenches.

> In the world of data, people often say "big," but very rarely "fresh."

Remember that story from Chapter 5 about video tracking in the English Premier League? During matches, special video cameras are tracking the players and ball at 25 frames per second, thus generating over 3 million data points per match.[3]

A few hours after the game is finished, the tracking data can be downloaded from the provider's website. Three million data points is too much to fit in a spreadsheet, but if you can write code, you can calculate various aggregate metrics easily enough.

One practical use for this data is monitoring players' physical outputs: distance covered, distance covered at high speed, number of sharp accelerations and decelerations, etc. The backroom staff of a football team may be interested in both the total output of each player as well as how it was changing throughout the game.

The shelf life of tracking data depends on how it is used:

- Historical analysis and research do not typically require recent data. You are more concerned with how far back your data goes, not if you have got data from yesterday's game. Data's shelf life is practically infinite. How quickly new data is obtained and processed does not matter.

- If the data helps decide how players train and recover the day after the game, it needs to be available some time before the recovery session starts. In this case, data's shelf life is likely to be between 12 and 24 hours. A manual process—download data, run calculations, present numbers and plots to stakeholders—may be time-consuming, but it gets the job done.

The above use-cases do not require a fully automated process. But the data provider also offers a real-time[4] data feed. This opens up another usage scenario:

- If players' outputs can be monitored *during* the game, it can facilitate decision-making with regards to recovery protocols at half-time ("Who needs an energy gel?") and full-time ("Who needs a protein shake and ice bath?"), and potentially even substitutions ("Has this player dropped off and needs to be taken off?").

In this situation, data "goes off" in a matter of minutes. A lag of 5 minutes may be acceptable, 10 minutes—not so much. Automation becomes crucial.

At Arsenal FC, we built a pipeline that delivers data from the provider to our infrastructure, where a lightweight script calculates several output metrics and pushes them to a live dashboard. Here is a simplified example with a single metric (unlabeled *y*-axis) plotted for nine players (also unlabeled) across a 90-minute game:

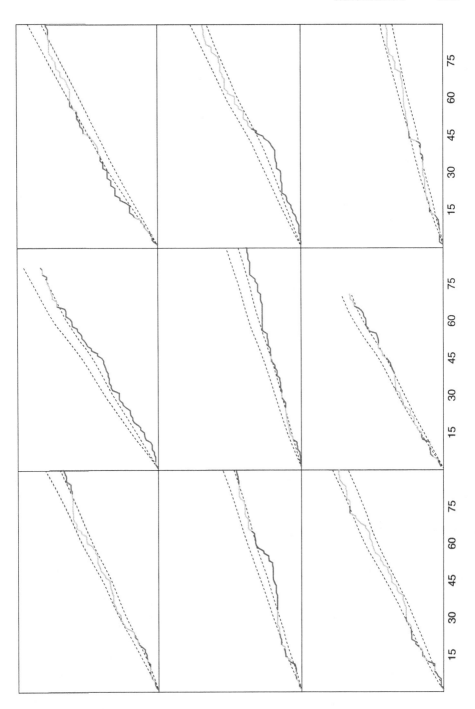

The cumulative output of each player is compared to expectations based on historical figures. The latter are shown as dashed lines: upper and lower bounds. When the in-game output goes outside the expected range, the line changes color to stand out.

You can only show a static picture in a book. In reality, these lines would be worming their way up and to the right as the game progressed. A quick look at the plot—and you can see both the big picture (which players have been running their socks off, and which are lagging behind) and the fine detail (each player's trajectory in time).

In terms of data science, this is nothing to write home about. This is just a collection of color-coded line plots showing a running total. The critical ingredient, without which it would be useless, is data delivery speed. And for speed, you need automation.

---

questions to consider

No matter how many benefits we can list, automation can still go wrong.

At the highest level, when considering automating a task, one should ask (1) if it should be automated at all, (2) when it would be the best time to implement automation, and (3) how it should be implemented. If, when, how.

If

Whatever it is you need to do with data, chances are it can be automated. But it is not a given that it should be. The engineering spirit that any good data scientist should possess eggs them on to build conveyor belts and robots. But with experience comes wisdom. And wisdom says, "Balance."

> With 2020/2021 football season having a tighter schedule due to you-know-what, I was asked to confirm the number of games Arsenal had to play during a certain period against the same period previous season.
>
> This might have looked like a trivial task, but the nature of data sources available to me at the time would make it more complicated. With the club having played in multiple competitions (English Premier League, two domestic cups, Europa League) and the Premier League having changed tracking data

provider,[5] there was not a readily available data set that would, with absolute certainty, contain every single game played across the periods I had to compare.

I was rolling up my sleeves thinking how I would go about getting accurate numbers, when I was struck by a brilliant idea: since this is a one-off question, and there were just a few dozen games to tally up, why don't we just "google" it[6]? That would take a few minutes maximum—no way I can do it faster using data.

The only downside was that it did not feel good to resort to such a "manual" approach. Looking at the screen and mouthing "one, two, three..." is so undignified. The pain was somewhat eased by my making the person who asked the question do it themselves.

One of my favorite XKCD comics does a great job of showing what happens when automation is the wrong approach:

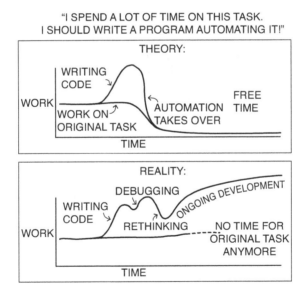

Everything has its cost and benefits. When you are considering automating a task, you already know the cost of performing the task manually. As for the hypothetical automated solution, you have to make estimations.

When you like automating things, it is easy to overestimate the benefits of an automated solution. It is a sort of "Halo effect": automation is pure good, and its benefits are plentiful. What is often overlooked is that everything is transient, everything comes to an end. I have done data science in different settings, and, with very few exceptions, most processes have had a very limited lifespan.

Let's say there is a task that takes you half an hour every week. It is a boring task, and you are itching to write code and forget about it. Half an hour every week sounds like a lot of time to be saved. But what if the business process is going to change in a year's time, and that task is going to be dropped or replaced? This immediately puts a cap on the time saved—at around 25 hours. Now we are talking about 3–4 working days. Can you develop a solution in a *significantly* shorter time? And what are the chances that maintaining that solution will not eat into the time savings?

Easy as it is to overestimate the benefits of automation, it is even easier to underestimate its costs: the time and effort that will go into writing and debugging code, putting it into production and maintaining it. Remember the optimism bias from Chapter 3?

I am often asked to do something "as soon as," and when I inquire as to whether this means that this new task is now my top priority, i.e., I should drop everything else, I get a response along the lines of "surely, that's a 20-minute job."

Even putting aside the issue of context switching, when you may spend 10–15 minutes just to get going on a new task and then, when it is done, another 10–15 to remember where you were on the previous one, 20 minutes is the *best-case scenario*.

Yes, sometimes the task does turn out to be trivial. Or you *made* it trivial by having written a high-quality code, which is easy to read and modify. But only sometimes. Other times, you run into an unexpected problem. Or problems. And then, before you know it, 20 minutes turn into 2 hours, or an all-nighter.

I try to avoid estimates shorter than half a day for anything more complex than changing a color on a plot. If I get it done in half an hour—no harm done. Underpromise and overdeliver!

When it comes to predicting how long a software development project will take, most of the time people end up being too optimistic. They overestimate their skills and underestimate the complexity of the problem. You cannot really know how difficult a problem is until you have solved it.

Sometimes you learn that a task is not worth automating in hindsight. You may even have reasons to "de-automate" it, if maintaining the automated solution turns out to take more time than doing the task manually. This is more likely to happen in an "unstable" environment, with frequent changes to data structure and/or requirements.

> I have gone through a phase when I was turning everything into an online dashboard. Even something that would be looked at once a month.
> Later on, having come to my senses, whenever I had to update the code behind a dashboard, I would think carefully if it might be better to just have a script that I would run on demand to generate a static report. If it is needed only once in a while, takes a minute, and running a script gives me more control over the end result, then—gasp!—automation may be an overkill.

When

Sometimes the question is not *if* a task should be automated, but *when*.

> Sometimes the question is not *if* a task should be automated, but *when*.

The story at the beginning of this chapter describes the gradual emergence of a full automation: from a very much manual process, through templates and scripts to a complete, lights-out solution. It was done according to Gall's law, which states: "A complex system that works is invariably found to have evolved from a simple system that worked. A complex system designed from scratch never works and cannot be patched up to make it work. You have to start over with a working simple system." (Gall, 1975).

If someone had attempted to leapfrog the first three phases and started working on a fully automated A/B test analysis process from day 1, they would most inevitably have wasted a lot of time and effort, and quite likely have had to abandon the idea until the time was right.

Before you consider automation, it is useful to get your hands dirty, get as close to the data as possible, and refrain from using anything that can obstruct your view of any step of the process. You need to understand the data and its idiosyncrasies, verify your assumptions and discover edge cases, get feedback from your end-users and fine-tune your output accordingly.

An analogy can be made with a data scientist's career. No matter how talented a fresh graduate is, it would be a silly move to hire them as a Chief Data Analytics Officer of a large company. No, first they should work as a Junior Data Scientist and learn the basics under the supervision of someone with experience. With time, they will

> The best path to automation is one that does not skip a step.

become a Senior Data Scientist, and it will be their turn to show the ropes and mentor. If they have the ambition and skills to manage others, they will take the next step and lead a team of data scientists. Having acquired enough knowledge and skills in the areas of data science and people management, as well as deep understanding of how the company works, this careerist of ours will eventually emerge as someone who can lead the data science efforts of the entire organization.

Just like this imaginary career path, the best path to automation is one that does not skip a step.

How

We have looked at the questions of *if* automation is needed, and *when* it should be done. Let's now look at *how*. This is not to discover a step-by-step guide to automation, but to illustrate that it can be done in ways that are extremely unequal.

In the context of data science, the quality of automation is very much synonymous with quality of code. A complex project that contains multiple parts would take us to the realm of software architecture, which deals with multiple software elements and how they interact with each other. This is too deep for a light book on data science, so let's limit ourselves to a single piece of code. Beyond a "Hello, world!" example,[7] any program can be written very badly or very well.

Once upon a time, a colleague of mine (not a data scientist) asked for help with her R script. She was trying to solve a problem, which was simple in the mathematical sense, but somewhat complex logistically.

She had to do some calculations on a large number of data files. In theory, she could do it using spreadsheets, but it was not a practically viable solution. She had limited experience with programming, but decided to try and automate the process using R.

Each data file contained a series of measurements in 3D space. Eight different variables for each of the three axes: X, Y, Z—24 variables in total:

	var1_x	var2_x	var3_x	var4_x	var5_x	var6_x	...	var3_z	var4_z	var5_z	var6_z	var7_z	var8_z
1	-21.0	-23.3	-24.0	-25.6	-21.8	-20.2		12.7	6.71	8.94	9.33	14.2	11.4
2	-25.8	-26.3	-27.2	-28.6	-25.5	-23.6		13.1	7.09	12.2	10.4	14.9	12.0
3	-30.8	-29.5	-30.5	-31.8	-29.2	-27.1		14.0	7.58	15.3	11.6	16.0	13.0
4	-33.8	-32.6	-33.8	-34.9	-32.3	-30.3		14.4	7.62	16.2	12.2	16.7	13.7
5	-36.7	-35.8	-37.2	-38.0	-35.2	-33.5		14.2	7.41	16.2	12.3	16.8	13.9
6	-40.3	-39.1	-40.8	-41.3	-38.5	-36.9		13.9	7.43	16.5	12.4	16.9	14.1
7	-43.8	-42.5	-44.3	-44.7	-41.9	-40.5		14.0	7.62	16.4	12.8	17.2	14.3
8	-47.3	-45.8	-47.7	-48.0	-45.2	-44.0		14.0	7.62	16.0	13.1	17.5	14.5
9	-50.8	-49.2	-51.1	-51.4	-48.6	-47.5		14.3	7.84	16.2	13.5	17.9	14.8
10	-54.3	-52.7	-54.7	-54.9	-52.0	-51.1		14.4	8.24	16.7	13.8	18.3	15.1

For each variable, she had to find the lowest measurement along the X axis and take the corresponding Y and Z values. She had written this code for the first variable:

```
minx1 <- min(data$var1_x)
index1 <- match(c(min(data$var1_x)), data$var1_x)
y1 <- data$var1_y[index1]
z1 <- data$var1_z[index1]
```

(If you are not familiar with R, do not worry about understanding the above code in detail. It can serve as a purely visual illustration.)

So far so good. It gets the job done. She copy-pasted this code for each of the remaining seven variables:

```
minx1 <- min(data$var1_x)
index1 <- match(c(min(data$var1_x)), data$var1_x)
y1 <- data$var1_y[index1]
z1 <- data$var1_z[index1]

minx2 <- min(data$var2_x)
index2 <- match(c(min(data$var2_x)), data$var2_x)
y2 <- data$var2_y[index2]
z2 <- data$var2_z[index2]

minx3 <- min(data$var3_x)
index3 <- match(c(min(data$var3_x)), data$var3_x)
y3 <- data$var3_y[index3]
z3 <- data$var3_z[index3]

minx4 <- min(data$var4_x)
index4 <- match(c(min(data$var4_x)), data$var4_x)
y4 <- data$var4_y[index4]
z4 <- data$var4_z[index4]

minx5 <- min(data$var5_x)
index5 <- match(c(min(data$var5_x)), data$var5_x)
y5 <- data$var5_y[index5]
z5 <- data$var5_z[index5]

minx6 <- min(data$var6_x)
index6 <- match(c(min(data$var6_x)), data$var6_x)
y6 <- data$var6_y[index6]
z6 <- data$var6_z[index6]
```

```
minx7 <- min(data$var7_x)
index7 <- match(c(min(data$var7_x)), data$var7_x)
y7 <- data$var7_y[index7]
z7 <- data$var7_z[index7]

minx8 <- min(data$var8_x)
index8 <- match(c(min(data$var8_x)), data$var8_x)
y8 <- data$var8_y[index8]
z8 <- data$var8_z[index8]
```

This approach had a few obvious shortcomings:

- There was a lot of code, and it was hard to read.
- She had to edit variable numbering every time she cloned the first chunk of code, multiplying opportunities for an error. And that error would be very hard to find afterwards.
- If she would have to modify her approach later on, she would have to meticulously change every chunk.

She then had to calculate the difference between every combination of metrics for each axis, which she achieved with a similarly repetitive approach:

```
list(
       x = c(
               minx1 - minx2, minx1 - minx3, minx1 - minx4,
               minx1 - minx5, minx1 - minx6, minx1 - minx7,
               minx1 - minx8,
               minx2 - minx3, minx2 - minx4, minx2 - minx5,
               minx2 - minx6, minx2 - minx7, minx2 - minx8,
               minx3 - minx4, minx3 - minx5, minx3 - minx6,
               minx3 - minx7, minx3 - minx8,
               minx4 - minx5, minx4 - minx6, minx4 - minx7,
               minx4 - minx8,
               minx5 - minx6, minx5 - minx7, minx5 - minx8,
               minx6 - minx7, minx6 - minx8,
               minx7 - minx8
       ),
       y = c(
               y1 - y2, y1 - y3, y1 - y4, y1 - y5, y1 - y6, y1
               - y7, y1 - y8,
               y2 - y3, y2 - y4, y2 - y5, y2 - y6, y2 - y7, y2
               - y8,
```

```
               y3 - y4, y3 - y5, y3 - y6, y3 - y7, y3 - y8,
               y4 - y5, y4 - y6, y4 - y7, y4 - y8,
               y5 - y6, y5 - y7, y5 - y8,
               y6 - y7, y6 - y8,
               y7 - y8
     ),
     z = c(
               z1 - z2, z1 - z3, z1 - z4, z1 - z5, z1 - z6, z1
               - z7, z1 - z8,
               z2 - z3, z2 - z4, z2 - z5, z2 - z6, z2 - z7, z2
               - z8,
               z3 - z4, z3 - z5, z3 - z6, z3 - z7, z3 - z8,
               z4 - z5, z4 - z6, z4 - z7, z4 - z8,
               z5 - z6, z5 - z7, z5 - z8,
               z6 - z7, z6 - z8,
               z7 - z8
     )
)
```

I actually found a typo (y5 instead of y6) when I was looking through the code, which showcased how well this approach lent itself to a mistake.

With all its shortcomings, the script worked. The problem my colleague was facing was that she had nearly a hundred data sets, and she was trying to copy-paste and modify this code for *each* data set. Having done it five or six times, she realized that it would take her until Christmas and decided to seek professional help.

* * *

First, I rewrote the script for processing a single data set. Since it was a one-off analysis, and code readability mattered little, I went for a compact solution:

```
lapply(
     1:8,
     function(i) {
               index <- which.min(data[[i]])
               set_names(
                    tibble(
                              data[index, i],
                              data[index, i + 8],
                              data[index, i + 16]
                    ),
```

```
                        c ("x", "y", "z")
                )
        }
) %>%
bind_rows () %>%
lapply (
        function(v) apply (
                combn (1:8, 2),
                MARGIN = 2,
                function (i) v [i [1]] - v [i [2]]
        )
)
```

As you can see, this is much less code to wrap one's head around, and it also contains much fewer numbers, which makes it far easier to QA.

With a few more lines of code, I had the script looping through the data files performing the same operation:

```
# previous code as a function
process_file <- function (file_name) {
        data <- read_csv (file_name)
        lapply (
                1:8,
                function (i) {
                        index <- which.min (data [[i]])
                        set_names (
                                tibble (
                                        data [index, i],
                                        data [index, i + 8],
                                        data [index, i + 16]
                                ),
                                c ("x", "y", "z")
                        )
                }
        ) %>%
        bind_rows () %>%
        lapply (
                function (v) apply (
                        combn (1:8, 2),
                        MARGIN = 2,
                        function (i) v [i [1]] - v [i [2]]
                )
        )
}
```

```
# apply function to each file
lapply(
        list.files("csv"),
        process_file
)
```

Now it did not matter if there were a hundred files or a thousand. The entire code fit on a laptop screen and saved my colleague many hours of grueling work.

And it was not that she had not tried to automate the original task. She had. It was just that her code did not go far from manual operations. It was as if she was trying to say "one hundred," but only knew the word "one" and had to go "one plus one plus one…"

Every chunk of the original script was equivalent to a set of a few manual operations in a spreadsheet and had to be repeated again and again. This kind of "automation" was disappointingly close to doing things by hand.

The magic of automation had to be applied to automation itself: instead of repeating a chunk of code, the latter had to be put inside a loop, which would run it as many times as needed. It was as if we needed to build a lot of robots, and instead of assembling them ourselves we built a robot that builds robots.

A sign of good automation is that it lasts.

Just like a building or a piece of furniture, well designed code will always outlive low-quality work.

A sign of good automation is that it lasts.

To quote a colleague of mine (a good software engineer himself), "One of the questions I ask a candidate in an interview is if there is any code they have written that is still running somewhere. Always a good sign if they can give at least one example."

Automation can be pure magic. Or a waste of time. It can be done beautifully and efficiently. Or so poorly that people will use it as a how-not-to guide. When all is said and done, automation is just a meta-tool; its usefulness depends on the people wielding it.

Automation is just a meta-tool; its usefulness depends on the people wielding it.

People are the subject of the next, and last, part of this book.

glossary

Edge case is a problem or situation that occurs only at an extreme operating parameter. In programming, an edge case may involve an input value that requires special handling.

Integrated development environment (IDE) is an application that facilitates writing the software code. A kind of text editor with additional functionality.

works cited

Systemantics: How Systems Really Work and How They Fail / p. 71 / John Gall / 1977 Quadragle/The New York Times Book Co.

notes

1 A manufacturing process that requires no human presence on-site.

2 The "10,000-hour rule" is a popular idea that the key to mastering a skill is to practice it for a total of around 10,000 hours $\simeq$ 5 years at 40 hours a week.

3 23 objects × 90 minutes × 60 seconds × 25 frames = 3,105,000.

4 Rather, "near real-time," with a typical lag of 2–3 minutes.

5 https://trainingground.guru/articles/second-spectrum-set-for-premier-league-debut.

6 https://www.google.com/search?hl=en&q=arsenal%20fixtures.

7 A program that displays the message "Hello, World!" is often used to illustrate the basic syntax of a programming language and is often the first written by someone learning it.

people, people, people

"Cadres are all-important," said Joseph Stalin in his speech in 1935. He was not everyone's cup of tea, but in this, he was right. ("Cadres" in this context is equivalent to "personnel.")

Part II of this book has covered data science best practices—how to align data science efforts with organization's needs and how to maximize their long-term returns. There was an assumption of a functioning data science team, but how do you build and maintain one?

This is a topic that deserves not even an entire book, but volumes. And there *are* volumes out there dedicated to creating and managing data science teams. The present book has a modest ambition to bring into light important topics that do not often come up in conversations.

Part III is dedicated to the main component of data science—people.

- Chapter 7 is about hiring the right people.
- Chapter 8 is about retaining the right people you have hired.
- Chapter 9 is about measuring people's performance.

As you might have already come to expect, it is not going to be a comprehensive guide, but rather an overview of common mistakes and how to avoid them, backed up by a few non-sugar-coated stories.

DOI: 10.1201/9781003057420-9

hiring a data scientist

The importance of hiring the right people varies from industry to industry, which is often reflected in the salary range. There is a reason why some jobs are paid minimum wage—no matter how good you are at it, you are relatively easy to replace with someone else who needs a job, any job. They may be not as good as you, but not by an order of magnitude.

Jobs that require experience and skills, e.g., a carpenter, are paid better. The supply of people who can do them is limited, and the market equilibrium shifts in favor of the employee. Furthermore, there is a much more pronounced difference between what is produced by a good carpenter and a bad one.

Things get even more interesting when we come to jobs whose output falls into the category of "intellectual property." Once again, let's look at software developers. If you hire one to develop an app, the result of their efforts may be used by hundreds, thousands, or millions of people, and the number of users does not necessarily inflate development costs. And, importantly, the quality of the code can be the difference between a best-selling app and a flop.

Whether or not you subscribe to the idea of a "10x developer," it is self-evident that even a modest difference in experience and aptitude of a software developer can result in a significant difference in the speed and quality of their work. Furthermore, a particularly challenging problem will have a threshold—a developer of insufficient "quality" will produce zero value in solving it.

DOI: 10.1201/9781003057420-10

As we discussed in Chapter 5 on quality assurance, the work of a data scientist may contain errors that are harder to discover than those in traditional software code. Data scientists often find themselves in a situation where they can get away with sloppy work, producing numbers and plots that do not reflect reality with any degree of accuracy, and which result in business decisions that are no better than those based on a hunch.

When it comes to data science, the quality of each and every person hired can have a decisive impact on the output of the entire team, and the impact of the team on the business. This chapter is concerned with hiring data scientists and may be especially useful for recruiters and hiring managers. It may also be useful for people who want to get hired, both data science candidates trying to break into the field and seasoned data scientists looking to advance their careers.

* * *

There are five components to a successful hiring process:

1. **Pain**:

    People in the organization are aware of a problem or set of problems that can be potentially solved using data science.

2. **Vision**:

    The hiring manager knows what it takes to solve these problems.

3. **Transmission**:

    Job requirements are reflected in the job advert and/or briefed to a recruiter.

4. **Urgency**:

    People involved in the hiring process realize that they are competing with other employers.

5. **System**:

    The hiring process is consistent and includes a feedback loop.

Let's discuss what can go wrong with each of the above, with some examples of what happens when it does.

pain

People in the organization are aware of a problem or set of problems that can be potentially solved using data science.

It would be naive to assume that whenever a company is hiring the only possible motivation behind it is that there is a job to be done. The best piece of advice for a cynical mid-level manager is this: "Figure out the baseline headcount growth rate for the company and grow your team at least as much."[1]

I have known data science managers whose career was essentially an ascending spiral with the following cycle at its core:

1. Join a company that vaguely wants to be data driven and has a hiring budget.
2. Talk enthusiastically to the company management about how data analytics is going to take them to the next level—without going into detail as to what the plan is exactly.
3. Put out job ads for data roles.
4. Talk enthusiastically to candidates about how they will be at the heart of transforming the business and having a real impact, and how they will be using the latest technology, doing machine learning and artificial intelligence. Again, do not go into detail.
5. Add another section to your CV about [establishing/growing/reorganizing] an analytics team and [driving/enabling/improving] various aspects of the business.
6. Wait for a better offer from another company.

This cycle is relatively short, typically below 2 years. If you stay with a company longer, you are risking actually doing something. Six to twelve months is just enough to make a few hires and make it look like a managerial job well done. Add a couple of months to land a new job, then a few more for the notice period.

People above (top-level management) or below (one of the hires) this job-hopping manager in the company hierarchy are not necessarily hurt in the process. They only suffer if they were taking the whole charade at face value and genuinely expected some useful work to be done. If they are not burdened with such sentiments, they can join the ride and advance their career with minimal effort.

In this scenario, data science does not address any problems. It is simply used as a front for the business of growing teams and people's careers. It is your choice whether or not to play this game, but given how far you are into this book, you probably want something more meaningful.

I was working in a small data analytics team when our team manager decided to accept an exciting offer from another company. (If anyone changes companies more often than a data scientist, then it is a data science manager.) The company failed to find an adequate replacement within the notice period, and people at the top decided to go with a consultant as a temporary solution.

A consultant in the role of a team manager is a dubious idea. They know they are leaving after the contract period. They are not going to get a promotion. Nor are they going to be fired, barring exceptional circumstances. They have no stake in the long-term success of the team. Unsurprisingly, our consultant spent most of his time sitting at his desk watching videos. I suspect that sometimes he would even nod off, which did not make much of a difference.

The consultant was tasked with hiring a data analytics team lead. We were sharing an office, so I could not help overhearing his side of several phone interviews. He would tell prospective candidates about the company and the position and ask them a few general questions—nothing unusual.

What was unusual, albeit not completely unexpected, was his attitude. I have never heard someone sound so bored in a phone interview. I could easily imagine that if I were the candidate on the other end, that conversation alone would have put me off.

Soon, this consultant left the company. I left, too, a couple of long months after. This story stuck with me as an excellent illustration of what happens when a lack of pain—and, therefore, willpower to do anything substantial—propagates down the chain of command. The people in charge of hiring a data science manager were going to be pain-free regardless of the performance of the person they would find, so they chose the path of least resistance. The consultant they hired could not possibly feel any pain either, and as a result the whole team was left adrift for months to come.

Occasionally, there is a genuine pain in the organization. There are problems that need to be solved, and there are people who believe that data science is the answer. This is more likely to happen in a small organization (or a small department), where people with the hiring power are close to the frontline.

An inkling of data science being a potential solution is a good start, but it is also important that people who initiate the hiring process understand what it is that data science can bring to the table. It would be reasonable to expect that a business leader has a good enough grasp on the business they are leading, but unless they have got a technical background, they may not understand well what data science can and can't do for it.

Too often people gravitate to one of the extremes: they see data science either as glorified accounting or as a kind of magic. In the former case, they are unlikely to invest enough in the recruitment of high-quality data scientists. In the latter, they may invest a lot, but also have unreasonable expectations as to how much and how quickly they can get in return. Disappointment is inevitable, and data science fades into the background—until the leadership changes and the cycle may repeat.

A balanced view of the potential of data science generally requires that the leadership group have at least one person with first-hand experience of working in a data-driven organization. They will play a key role in establishing data science's place in the organization and managing expectations.

Only a genuine pain and understanding of how data science can alleviate it will create the will to invest in data science, which will propagate down the company hierarchy. To succeed in hiring, the person who initiates it needs to "want it bad".

> To succeed in hiring, the person who initiates it needs to "want it bad."

---

vision

The hiring manager knows what it takes to solve these problems.

We humans are aiming creatures. We have an extremely focused vision that allows us to zoom in on a target. Our language reflects that. We always talk about our targets, our aims, our goals. We need a goal, otherwise we have no idea where we are and where to go. We are at point A and we do not like it. We see or imagine point B, and it looks better than point A. Done—point B is our goal now.

Our not liking it at point A is exactly the pain we talked about before. For example, a company has been collecting data from its business processes, but there is no-one who has got the skill set and/or time to use it towards improving the bottom line. An executive imagines point B: there is a data analyst who crunches the data and brings insights into the company leadership. A goal is born.

"We need someone to crunch the data" is a vague goal. The vision of exactly how it is going to help the business is blurry. If the hiring process gets kicked off based on this vision, then the probability that the right candidate will be identified and hired is low. What skill set does someone need to successfully "crunch the data"? What kind of academic background and work experience?

"We need someone who can develop a set of business KPI's and build a data-driven report" is a sentence that is only marginally longer, but it already provides some direction as to what kind of candidate the company should be looking for. A business analyst proficient with spreadsheets and SQL could be a good start. Perhaps someone with experience of putting together a self-serving data tool. A PhD in machine learning is probably not a must-have.

* * *

A blurry vision makes for an awkward hiring process. I have been in both roles, interviewer and interviewee, when the interview had no clear goal. It is no good for either side. As the interviewer, you try your best to ask questions because you know that is what an interviewer does, but you do not really understand why you are asking them, and how the candidate's responses should be shaping your decision. As the interviewee, you may or may not be aware of what is going on, but you definitely cannot help the interviewer in their task of determining whether or not you are a good fit.

My first experience as interviewer came when I was working as a customer support representative at a software company. Alongside another relatively experienced team member, I was tasked to interview a candidate, a young gentleman aspiring to be employed.

Neither my colleague nor I really knew how to conduct an interview. As a support engineer with a couple of years under my belt, I had a good idea of what the job entailed, but I was unable to draw connections from that to what skills or personal qualities we were looking for, or from the latter—to what we would want to find out about the candidate.

"Fake it till you make it," we did exactly that. We asked a few generic questions and offered a couple of logical puzzles—"to assess candidate's overall intelligence." Unsurprisingly, these questions did little to help us. In the end, we decided not to hire, because we just did not like the candidate's "vibe."

It took me some time to realize, in hindsight, what exactly went wrong with that interview. While we felt the pain—the team was understaffed—we lacked a clear vision of what we were looking for, therefore had no goal, no direction in conducting the interview. Like parrots, we would utter questions we had heard before, with no intelligence behind them.

To have a clear vision, the interviewer needs to know—in no vague terms—why the company is looking for another data scientist. If they know that, they will know what qualities make a great candidate, and will be able to ask questions that will help them see whether or not the candidate has these qualities.

Furthermore, with a clear goal in mind, the interviewer will have a much easier time answering the candidate's questions (a good interview is a two-way street). If you know what you need another data scientist for, you will be able to answer any question without hesitation:

- "What will be the first project I work on?"
- "How much does experience with machine learning matter?"
- "Who are the stakeholders, and how will I interact with them?"

As an absolute bonus, a clear vision makes it easier to compose the job ad and/or brief a recruiter.

---

transmission

Job requirements are reflected in the job advert and/or briefed to a recruiter.

Unless the hiring manager knows someone who miraculously combines meeting the job requirements and looking for a job, the company has to put out a job ad and/or have a recruiter start looking for potential candidates.

First thing to be said about data science job ads is that they have a low hit rate. Good candidates have enough options from just having a LinkedIn profile. They have no reason to look at job ads, which end up being a big investment with a low return.

Second thing to be said about data science job ads is that most of them suck.

To write a good job ad, one needs to

- know what job the new person will be doing (and this can change in the future);
- know what skills and experience that job requires;
- know how to write (a very much underappreciated skill);
- have the authority to post the ad as they have written it.

These, if present within the company at all, virtually never combine in a single person.

Once upon a time I worked with a manager who had his own consultancy company. The company claimed to "solve data challenges for businesses."

At one point he approached me asking to help write up a job ad for a data scientist position. "What requirements should I put in the job ad?" was, in a nutshell, his question.

I did help, of course, but I could not help thinking to myself, "If you don't know what skills you're looking for, how do you even know that you need a data scientist?"

In a well-functioning organization, the hiring manager (e.g., data science team lead) may have a good idea of the job at hand and what the requirements are. They are much less likely to be a good copywriter—it is a rare occurrence even among professional copywriters. And even if they want to compose a good job ad and know how to do it, they will probably be confronted by the HR department with their red tape.

Most of the time, the job ad is written by a somewhat random person, who may or may not have gone through the trouble of talking to the hiring manager in order to learn everything there is to learn about the job and what it entails. The ad contains a number of vague phrases, to which most candidates will mentally respond "yeah, sure, I can be that":

- team player,
- not afraid to roll up their sleeves,
- able to learn quickly,
- ready to work in a fast-paced environment,
- ...

Oftentimes, a poorly designed ad also lists every single tool and technology the future data scientist may conceivably come in contact with. Of course, it would be great if the data scientist could double as a data engineer, had years of experience with R, Python *and* another language for the sake of variety, did a PhD in computer vision... all in addition to outstanding people skills. When a job ad describes a superhero, it mostly attracts two categories of candidates:

- candidates who *are* superheroes, and who will probably get disappointed with what the company can offer (all these skills do not come cheap)—these will be few;
- candidates who are applying to as many positions as they can—these will be many.

Even if you do manage to find a superhero data scientist, who not only meets the requirements but is also happy with what the company can offer, things will quickly go sour when they realize that their advanced skills are not needed. Being overqualified is low on a data scientist's wish-list.

In this case, "less" can definitely be "more." An ad with a concise list of requirements, which are actually relevant to the job, may not protect you from candidates who apply to every position they find, but it will increase the proportion of candidates whom you may want to talk to.

When I was starting out as a data scientist in 2013, Hadoop (a software framework for distributed storage and processing of big data) was all the rage. It was a keyword that would get anyone's CV to the top of the pile.

A few years on, companies began to realize that, while they needed someone with a good knowledge of Hadoop to set everything up, the importance of that particular expertise plummeted once the system was up and running. The entry level to *using* Hadoop is low. Furthermore, alternative solutions were coming onto the market, and a data engineer familiar with a broad range of technologies was much more useful than a narrow Hadoop expert. Experience in building and maintaining a "data lake" came to be appreciated above the command of a specific framework.

Nowadays, with more and more companies moving to the "cloud," having own data lake is going out of fashion, and with it so is the importance of corresponding data warehousing skills.

Employers who are paying attention are evolving to appreciate candidates' general skills and "cultural fit," over expertise in specific technology. If the latter is desperately needed, it makes sense to find a consultant.

The field of data science brings the additional challenge of fuzzy job titles. What one company calls business analyst, another calls data analyst, while yet another decides to spice it up and go for data scientist. And titles do matter. A candidate proficient with SQL and spreadsheets will feel comfortable applying for a position of business analyst, but may shy away from the same job ad if it says "data scientist." And, vice versa, someone may feel their knowledge of R and Python makes them over-qualified for a position of business analyst, while they would be perfectly happy to apply for the same position, only titled "data scientist." On the other hand, some people are driven by what they think they should be called and may be put off by a modest job title, feeling they deserve more.

To make matters worse, as the area of data science is still evolving, many companies come up with new job titles. This is partly done to make positions more attractive, partly to avoid clashes with existing roles.

A fashion company announced a position of "Principal AI Architect" and, to their surprise, received no applications. The title was too fanciful, too unusual, and discouraged potential candidates from applying. In the end, the company had to fall back to something more familiar, and normal service resumed.

There are few companies that can get by just by leveraging their high profile and/or a referral program. (A referral program is generally just a bonus paid out to an existing employee for referring someone they know or pretend that they know for an open position. There is no fine for referring an unsuitable candidate.) A recruiter, whether internal or external, may be a necessary evil. Someone has to be put on the phone and start making those phone calls (or, more realistically, try and connect with potential candidates on LinkedIn).

The problem with a recruiter is that he or she will always find *someone*. If the recruiter is good, i.e., they know what they are doing, they understand what the company is looking for, and they know how to find the right person, then a satisfying outcome is feasible. But if the recruiter is a bit rubbish, they will still find a candidate and try to "sell" him or her, whether or not it is in the interests of the company.

Good fit or not, once the new hire has been at the company for a certain number of months (which may be necessary for the recruiter to get a full pay-out), the recruiter has no direct incentive for the hire to stay there any longer. The recruiter's top-line is driven by how often they match a candidate and a job, not by how long the formers stays in the latter, or how many projects they get over the line, or how happy they are. This creates an unhealthy motivation for recruiters to try and get as many people as they can to make a move.

The situation is exacerbated by the fact that it may be beneficial for the data scientist, too, to change jobs rather often. In my experience, it only happened once that I got a sizeable raise while staying with the same company, and it happened thanks to an exceptional manager. It is almost always easier to get a raise and/or promotion by moving to a different company. It is not uncommon for someone to leave the company only to re-join it a few months later, having had an opportunity to negotiate a raise twice. Meanwhile, their colleagues who decided to stay put are likely to only have had their yearly 2%–3%—inflation-level—salary increase.

* * *

A large company will have their own team of recruiters, each of them flipping through dozens if not hundreds of applications every day. Typically, they will spare around 30 seconds per application, taking a well-practiced glance at the list of skills and recent experience, looking for keywords.

This approach would not be too bad if all candidates used the same template for their CV. Which is not the case. The Internet offers a variety of templates, and some candidates channel their creativity (which is not always a bad idea). The same content can have a drastically different impact on a recruiter depending on how it is structured and styled.

The average jobseeker has no idea about how quickly their carefully crafted Word document will be judged. A typical CV is an eclectic mix of information that a recruiter is interested in and irrelevant things like:

- work experience from the beginning of time, including whatever they got up to in the last summer at university;
- unnecessarily detailed descriptions ("used Microsoft Excel 2010 to edit and save spreadsheets");
- hobbies—if they are relevant for the job, then it makes sense to list them as side projects, otherwise no-one cares.

As a result, the recruiter is screening not only (or even not so much) for matching skill set and relevant experience, but also for prowess in creating a concise, straight-to-the-point resume.

When I was part of the recruitment process, I would be asked to conduct a technical interview with data scientist candidates. I would receive their CV before the interview and, in the beginning, carefully study it.

After the first few candidates I noticed that the CV was a poor predictor of how the interview would go. A candidate with a mediocre CV could turn out to be very capable and keen, and we would have an engaging conversation, while someone with an impressive CV full of achievements could make me think, "If I can barely suffer though a 45-minute conversation with this person, I cannot imagine it being good to have them as a full-time colleague."

In the end, I decided to forego looking at the candidate's CV altogether and just focus on the 45 minutes I had with them face-to-face. I never had a cause to regret that decision. Everyone who got hired with my involvement became a valuable member of the data science team.

Of course, everyone's CV would still have been looked at as part of the HR screening process, and obviously unfit candidates would not have made it through to an in-person interview. But as long as a candidate's CV makes sense at all, I would argue that it loses its relevance for the rest of the hiring process.

And if an external recruiter may be driven by hidden incentives, the problem with internal recruiters is that they may have no incentives altogether. As long as then funnel in a reasonable number of candidates, no-one will have any reason to doubt their diligence.

> If an external recruiter may be driven by hidden incentives, the problem with internal recruiters is that they may have no incentives altogether.

urgency

People involved in the hiring process realize that they are competing with other employers.

When looking for a data scientist, most companies have to balance two goals:

- attract good candidates,
- assess candidates to pick the best one.

Too often, the hiring process is skewed towards the assessment part. From the very beginning, the focus is on finding out whether or not a candidate is a good fit, with no thought spared for making sure that candidates that *would* be a good fit would be interested in the position in the first place:

- A recruiter or HR person makes the initial phone call. They give a brief overview of the company and the job. They cannot go into anything technical, as they simply do not know enough. That would have to involve the hiring manager, and it is rarely done at this stage. Instead, the candidate is asked questions about their current salary and salary expectations. He or she is yet to have a reason to want the position, but already finds themselves in something akin to a negotiation.
- There is a technical test, either on-site or take-home, which may require from a couple of hours to a few evenings of the candidate's spare time. Arguably, a good way to assess a candidate, but even a better way to filter out the less desperate candidates and those with a busy life. As a friend of mine—a recruiter and a football fan—put it, "Would Arsenal invite a Jadon Sancho to try out at the training ground?"
- A grueling interview process, typically with people from different departments. Again, the focus is seldom on "selling" the job to the candidate, but on looking for "red flags."

Data science is a field with competitive hiring, at all levels of seniority. A data scientist with just a year or 2 of industry experience already attracts recruiters. And this is when they are *not* actively looking for new opportunities. Someone determined to find a new job is likely to be talking to several prospective employers at any given time.

Everyone understands that the purpose of the hiring process is to assess candidates. But not everyone understands that there is another purpose—to attract good candidates. There are a few data science positions that sell themselves, the rest have to be sold. If you do not attract good candidates in the first place, rigorous assessment will not fix it. A mistake

> If you do not attract good candidates in the first place, rigorous assessment will not fix it.

many companies make is that they try to assess candidates before the latter have been "hooked."

If the hiring company has successfully identified a reasonably small number of seemingly fit candidates, it will be a good idea to have them have a conversation with the hiring manager as soon as possible. This has two major benefits:

- The hiring manager is in the best position to answer a candidate's questions about the team, the projects it works on, and the role being hired for. This is exactly what a candidate needs to know to decide whether or not they want to pursue the opportunity.

- The candidate will also know that their time is not being wasted, as opposed to getting a phone call from a recruiter, who spends most of the call talking about themselves and the company they represent, and ends the conversation by asking the candidate to email them a CV, often never to get back.

A conversation with the hiring manager is an excellent way to kick off the hiring process. Next step is to ensure the hiring process takes as little time as possible. If someone is looking for a new job, they are almost certainly looking in several places. Unless your company sits at the top of the job market food chain, most candidates will probably go with whoever makes an acceptable offer first. It *is* a race.

Early 2013. I have applied for my first data scientist job—with a small, but ambitious gaming company named King. I have done well in the on-site test and was awaiting a round of interviews.

There was a complication, of a good sort. I have received another job offer. It was not as attractive, and I would have to move to another city, but it was the proverbial bird in hand. The only thing remaining was to put my signature on the contract, and I could only delay it by another day or two. A predicament.

I did the only thing I could think of—show up at King's office, ask for Magnus (the hiring manager), and describe the situation to him. It worked. I was rushed through several in-person and remote interviews in a single day and got the job.

It worked because the company was still small and agile. It would never have worked a couple of years later, when King had several times the headcount, a sizeable recruitment team, and a much more rigid hiring process in place. Last I heard, it consisted of six (!) stages, one of which was a technical test that takes a weekend.

Now, if you are desperate for a job and have not got many options to choose from, you will probably wait around for a few weeks, no problem. But if you are an experienced data scientist with a solid CV, chances are you are getting messages from recruiters on a regular basis, and, if you are actively looking for new opportunities, you are also getting offers. Employers do not always realize that they are competing with others. Good candidates have multiple options.

> Employers do not always realize that they are competing with others. Good candidates have multiple options.

This results in the wrong kind of filter: by taking too long to funnel candidates through the hiring process, the company filters out the better candidates, who accept an offer from a company with a more efficient process, and filters in the candidates who have been able to wait around—for the reason of not being as attractive to other potential employers.

---

system

The hiring process is consistent and includes a feedback loop.

Many of us probably do a better job choosing a toaster than deciding whether or not to hire a candidate. Understandably, too:

- We have got a better idea of what exactly we need: how many slots, additional features, how easy to clean, etc.
- It is probably not the first toaster we are buying, and we remember what went right or wrong with those we have had.
- We can pick our favorite color, and no-one is going to judge us.

I am sure there are organizations and people who have devised a neat checklist and a simple grading system, so that they can compare candidates in a fair and objective way. I have not met those people.

The hiring discussions I have seen were very normal, run-of-the-mill conversations, in which several interviewers would offer their fuzzy opinions and eventually settle on a yes-or-no decision. This approach would be enough for a casual toaster purchase, but you would think that an important hiring decision would have more solid foundations.

As many data scientists, at one point of my career I had an interview at Facebook. Rather, a round of interviews, mostly with data scientists and engineers, which I liked. I was not at all sure if I would want to work at Facebook, but I felt that the interviews went well and was curious to see what kind of offer I would get.

Weeks passed, and no-one got back to me. I was not very keen on the move, so I did not try and follow up. A few months later, purely by chance, I ran into the recruiter at the office of another company, to which he had moved from Facebook. He remembered me, and I asked him if there was a particular reason why I had not got an offer. He could not remember all the details, but he did remember that one of the interviewers thought it was strange that during the interview I had to use the bathroom.

I am not claiming that little incident was the *main* reason why I was not deemed a good fit but hearing that it was even mentioned was an interesting insight into Facebook's hiring process.

* * *

A few years later, I got a message from another Facebook recruiter, who was hiring for senior data scientist positions. She wrote in her message, "You interviewed with us before, and there was some really positive feedback."

That message left me scratching my head—had I been not good enough then, but they have dropped their standards? Or do they expect me to have become a better data scientist since then, and they are ready to give me another chance?

If someone asked me for a single most important piece of life advice (this happened just once so far), I would say, "Whatever you do, make sure there is a feedback loop."

In its simplest explanation, when we have got a process with inputs and outputs, a feedback loop is making the outputs available as part of the inputs:

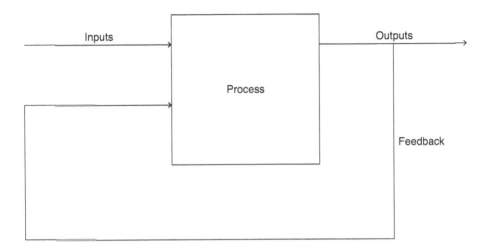

This is how, without exaggeration, all life works. A life form exhibits a behavior (inputs), analyzes what happens as result of that behavior (outputs) and uses it to adjust its behavior (feedback). Touch fire → get burned → do not touch fire again.

A system without a feedback loop is limited in its ability to improve. If you are doing something and you do not know how well it is working, how are you supposed to know if you need to change anything and in what direction?

Yet this is what a typical hiring process is. Everyone involved is providing an input: the recruiter screens applications, various people interview the candidates who have made it through, a collective decision is made. The output of this process is the impact of the new hire *and* the loss of potential impact of candidates who were passed on.

Most companies do some kind of a review at the end of the new hire's probation period (typically 3 or 6 months). Thus, some of the output is measured. The employee either stays on or does not. But this measurement is not fed back into the hiring process. There is no "post mortem" meeting of everyone who has been involved in the initial hiring decision. No-one asks, "Have we done a good job hiring this person? What could we have done better?"

And this only concerns people who have been hired. What about the more numerous category—candidates who have been passed on? It is, of course, more difficult to judge a no-hire decision, as those people move on to work somewhere else, but, in the world with LinkedIn, it would be easy enough to see how their career has developed in the following year or two. Whether they joined a well-known company and became a senior data scientist within a year or went down a different career path altogether would be a useful piece of feedback.

> A few months after I joined King, I referred two former colleagues from my previous company for a data scientist position. I held them both in high esteem and expected them to breeze in.
>
> First one made quite an impression on one of the interviewers by doing mental arithmetic while assembling a Rubik's cube. (Not that it was his most valuable skill.) He deservedly got the job and quickly became one of the best performers in the team. A clear win.
>
> The second one did not make as strong an impression in his interviews and was turned down as "a bit too junior," even though I vouched that he was definitely less "junior" than I was. He stayed with his old company, became employee of the month soon after, and a team lead a couple of years later. In my opinion, a *faux pas* by King's recruitment.

There cannot be a universal hiring process that would be optimal for everyone. However, if a company wants to have a shot at improving their hiring process, they must adhere to two principles:

- **Consistency**: have a structure to how candidates are attracted and assessed, and do not tweak, let alone revolutionize it without a good reason.
- **Feedback loop**: follow up on candidates, both hired and passed on, and look into the reasons behind "false positives" (hired, but should not have been) and "false negatives" (not hired, but should have).

P. S. underappreciated qualities

A clear vision will help you focus on the relevant skills and experience of a candidate and ask them the right questions. Knowing what kind of problems they will have to solve, you will be able to determine if they will be up to the task. At least, in terms of so-called "hard skills": statistics, programming, and so on. Evaluation of "soft skills" may be a tougher challenge.

There are certain skills and personal qualities that are routinely underappreciated:

Written Communication

Verbal communication skills are usually gauged well enough in interviews. Most people will consciously or unconsciously pick up on whether or not they are having trouble talking to the candidate. But verbal communication skills do not always reflect written communication skills, and the latter can be very important for a data scientist.

A data analysis report or presentation require the data scientist to convey their findings and thoughts, which may concern complex issues and ambiguous results, in a very careful, well thought-out manner. That said, even a short email, when written sloppily, may waste an incredible amount of time if people read it differently and get sucked into an unproductive discussion or, even worse, silently draw wrong conclusions.

We should never ever underestimate how easily written communication can be misinterpreted. And it happens even with people you would least expect to get it wrong.

Two days before World War II broke out in Europe, British Prime Minister sent a letter to Hitler, with the intention to make it clear that Britain would declare war if Germany invaded Poland. The letter was phrased in polite "diplomatese," and Hitler understood it as conciliatory. On September 1, 1939, the German tanks rolled.

> When we think that our words are perfectly clear and can only be misunderstood by an idiot, we are probably being idiots ourselves.

When we think that our words are perfectly clear and can only be misunderstood by an idiot, we are probably being idiots ourselves.

Speaking of email, it is one of the most important skills that is not taught in any systematic way. Coincidentally, the best manager I ever had as a data scientist started out by giving each data scientist in our team a few books he considered a must-read (and they were). Arguably, the most important one was *The Pyramid Principle: Logic in Writing and Thinking* (2009), which was all about communicating your ideas clearly and succinctly.

A good way to test a candidate's writing skills is to ask them to write about themselves as part of the job application process, for example, in a cover letter. A quick glance at what they wrote would reveal a lot:

- Have they put some effort into it, or does it look like a template off the Internet?
- Are they saying anything relevant, or is it all clichés and platitudes?
- Do they care more about the reader or about sounding smart?

It does not have to be perfect, but it is useful to imagine how you would feel if you had to read something similar every working day.

Goal Orientation

Many a job ad lists "goal oriented" or "result oriented" as a desirable quality in a candidate. It is not a quality that is easy to assess. Luckily, it does not matter—nobody actually tries to.

Most workers, data scientists included, are primarily paid for showing up. Yes, you do need to do a little show-and-tell every now and again. Sometimes there is a deadline to meet. Yet, most of the time, as long as you look busy, there is no life-or-death incentive to *solve a problem* as quickly as possible.

Unless you find yourself in an unusual situation, when there is someone who both cares about how efficient you are and knows how to gauge it (e.g., an ex-data scientist team lead), you may even be incentivized to work more slowly. The longer you take to complete a project, the harder it will seem to others, and the more time you will be given for a similar project in the future.

It is very difficult to create an environment that rewards efficiency in doing data science. We will talk more about it in Chapter 9. As far as hiring and managing data scientists are concerned, being goal oriented is a quality praised on paper, but rarely assessed and nurtured.

There is a semi trick question that allows a glimpse into how people reason about achieving a goal:
— Ideally, when should a task be completed?
Most people will either avoid giving a direct answer or answer with a question of their own. An experienced person may say, "By the deadline, of course!"
The correct answer is, "Now."

In the ideal world, whatever result we are looking for, we have already got it. In the real world, it does happen sometimes—perhaps there is a ready-made solution which we simply had forgotten about. Perhaps, we do have the resources to get what we need instantaneously. Probably not. What matters is that if we ask ourselves, "What stops us from getting it right now?" we will not be thinking specs, tasks, or features. Instead, we will be identifying and solving the biggest problems that stand between us and the desired outcome.

A data scientist with a "What stops us from getting the result right now?" mindset is precious. Even if they are lacking in hard skills, they will quickly pick up whatever they need to solve the problem. But goal orientation is *not* something you can easily pick up. Or instil into others.

Conscientiousness

A desire to do a task well, and to take obligations to others seriously is crucial for a data scientist working on their own or in a small team. Unless a data scientist is working in a sizeable team with other data scientists, or more generally, people who can hold them accountable, they need above-average self-discipline and work ethics.

I have worked as a lone data scientist embedded in a business team as well as in a small (2–3 people) data science team, and I know first-hand that it is easy to

- get isolated from other parts of the organization,
- work on fun projects that have little business value,
- inflate complexity of and time needed for a task.

When hiring their first (second, third) data scientist, a company should heavily prioritize conscientiousness. Without it, whatever skills the data scientist has may not be put to good use.

Empathy

This one may come as a surprise, especially in a field that is supposed to value hard facts, logic and rational thinking.

A data scientist almost always has to deliver results to someone who is *not* a data scientist. Someone who may look at the subject of data analysis and argue about it from a very different angle. Frustration with people "not getting" what they are talking about is not uncommon among data scientists.

Lacking empathy, a data scientist—typically, an intelligent and educated individual—may look down on people less versed in abstract thinking, probability theory, and so on. Business stakeholders often struggle to consume the end product of data science. Rather than alleviating their discomfort, an unempathetic data scientist will treat them with disdain, which only hurts the good will and overall credibility of data science in the organization.

Collecting feedback and understanding why people disagree with you is a crucial skill for the supporting role data scientists usually play. If a data scientist cannot find a common ground with stakeholders and get everyone behind a shared vision, they will be severely limited in the impact they can have, if any at all.

P. P. S. overappreciated qualities

There are two qualities that are overappreciated, often subconsciously, to an extent that warrants an addendum to this already overlong chapter.

Charisma

This encapsulates everything that makes a person more attractive and charming, particularly when it comes to the first impression. Good fashion sense, a firm handshake, effortless small talk... "What's wrong with all that?" you may ask.

There is nothing wrong with being charismatic in itself. But if you happen to come across two data scientists who have been equally successful in their career, and one of them is more charismatic than the other, you can be certain that the less charismatic data scientist has been successful *in spite of* their lacking charisma, which makes it very likely that they are a better data scientist than their charismatic counterpart.

Other things being equal, it makes sense to defy your first impression and go for the "ugly duckling" option — they have had to work harder.

> Other things being equal, it makes sense to defy your first impression and go for the "ugly duckling" option—they have had to work harder.

Confidence

People easily mistake confidence for competence, especially if they are not experts in the domain and cannot see if they are being "played." We find it much easier to rely on someone with strong opinions, stated loud and clear. Just look at any politician.

The job of a data scientist is to deal with complex issues, which often do not have a simple answer. He or she needs to be comfortable with saying "I don't know," "I am not sure," "We need to investigate it further." A businessperson, a decision-maker will press a data scientist for a quick binary answer, yes or no. Anything else will be viewed as mincing words and lacking confidence.

> I once had a performance review where I was told that I should be more confident in offering my opinion to stakeholders. "Don't just tell them what the data shows, tell them what you think they should do!"
>
> My argument was that it was important to draw a clear line between objective data and my subjective opinion. By offering the two as a package, I could easily mislead my audience to believe that my opinion was the only viable point of view based on the data, and that they should refrain from making their own judgment.
>
> As long as my audience understood the data-based findings I had presented, my opinion was no more valuable than anyone else's.

As Charles Bukowski said, "The problem with the world is that the intelligent people are full of doubts, while the stupid ones are full of confidence."

Socrates claimed to know nothing. He would struggle to make a career in today's corporate world, where the balance between epistemic humility and confidence in one's opinion is too often skewed towards the latter.

---

glossary

10x developer is a software developer who is considered to be as productive as ten average developers.

works cited

The Pyramid Principle / Barbara Minto / 2009 *Financial Times* / Prentice Hall.

note

1. Slava Akhmechet, "How to Get Promoted," https://www.spakhm. com/p/how-to-get-promoted.

what a data scientist wants

Hiring the right person is a good start. However, if this right person leaves the company before they have made an impact that justifies all the effort put in their recruitment, the entire campaign has been a bit of a failure.

While hiring and onboarding a new employee usually goes towards someone's KPI (recruiter, HR team, and hiring manager), failing to *retain* a valuable employee is rarely recognized as anyone's fault. And when I say "rarely" what I mean is that I have never even heard of someone being held responsible for employee turnover.

Data science is a field in which a few months of experience can make a big difference in both perceived and actual value of someone plying the trade. I cannot remember all examples of a new data scientist joining a company, getting their feet wet, and within a year or 2 departing for greener pastures—I have witnessed it too many times. It is never good for the company, but it rarely hurts anyone in particular enough for them to try and do anything about it. No-one is going to lose their yearly bonus. If anything, with a productive data scientist having left, there is an opportunity to kick off the recruitment process once again and keep a few people looking busy.

Intuitively, keeping someone already working for the company ought to be easier and cheaper than finding an adequate replacement. No matter the experience, everyone needs at least a couple of months, if not longer, to get up to speed at a new place. Counter-intuitively, most companies are more focused on attracting new talent than on keeping the existing talent content.

> Most companies are more focused on attracting new talent than on keeping the existing talent content.

DOI: 10.1201/9781003057420-11

So, how is one to keep data scientists happy and productive? What does a data scientist want from and on their job?

Any human endeavor is fundamentally about setting a goal, achieving that goal, and reaping the rewards:

This is how we get the dopamine hit. This is what enables us to go to work every day and, if we are lucky, even *want* to go.

As a data scientist, no matter your experience, whether you are research- or product-oriented, working on well-defined projects or "operational," one way or another you find yourself in the cycle of goal → achievement → reward. It is so fundamental. It is not about being a data scientist. It is not even about being a human. It is about being a living organism. That said, let's look at a data scientist's needs according to this framework.

goal

The need for a goal is deeply ingrained in our psychology and biology. All organizations I have been a part of would have some kind of goal framework. Something to answer the question of "What am I doing here?" on Monday morning.

Working on this book, I conducted an informal survey among the data scientists I know. Far from proper scientific research, it is nonetheless a valuable addition to my own experience. One thing the survey showed is that "unclear goals" is the second biggest source of frustration, with over 40% of respondents choosing it out of 16 options provided (they were allowed to select up to three options).

Setting a clear goal is not the end of it though. There are two components without which even a well-specified goal is likely to fail to motivate a data scientist: purpose and challenge.

Purpose

While goal specifies *where* we want to go, purpose specifies *why*. In a business setting, there is no need to make it a deep philosophical "why." It is enough to connect it to a high-level business goal, which is self-explanatory enough.

In my early days as a data scientist, I would not question the purpose of a project that was handed to me. The novelty of working with data was enough. I was happy as a puppy fetching the ball again and again.

As the number of finished projects under my belt was growing, simply doing data science was getting less satisfying on its own. The need to know *why* was getting stronger by the day.

One type of data science project I had to do more than once (not all at the same company) was so-called user segmentation—dividing the user base into several segments based on a number of characteristics (e.g., paying customers vs non-paying, casual gamers vs hardcore, etc.)

First time I was asked to do it, I was chuffed to bits just to try my hand at clustering algorithms. (Side note: real life is often disappointingly void of well-defined clusters. What I would always find was more akin to a bowl of clumpy porridge, which I could arbitrarily segment any way really.)

Second time I was still happy to do it, if anything just to utilize the experience I acquired figuring it out first time around.

When I found myself facing a user segmentation project for a third time, I was unable to stop myself from asking, "Actually, what are we going to use the user segments for?" The discussion that followed did not bring about a clear sense of purpose, and the project was put on hold. Last time I heard, it was simply given to another data scientist after I left the company.

We are talking about a data scientist's needs right now but clarifying the purpose behind a goal may have a highly beneficial side-effect. The data scientist will be making better-informed decisions working towards the goal.

For example, I may be asked to put together a data visualization based on data that has been collected daily for several years. This is a clear enough goal. I can put my head down, produce an interactive report and get a well-deserved pat on the back.

I can also invest five minutes into asking questions about who and how is going to use the report. I may find out that its purpose is two-fold: (1) look at yesterday's data to make quick decisions in the morning, and (2) explore historical data looking for trends. The first purpose would be better served by a lightweight one-page app that only shows most recent data and highlights unusually high and low values. The second warrants a more complex tool with multiple interactive plots—speed and ease-of-use are less of a concern now.

By developing two separate tools, which will not necessarily require more time and can even make future maintenance easier, I can satisfy each need better than if I had started working towards the goal without understanding the purpose.

Challenge

Another thing to get right when assigning a project to a data scientist is the level of *challenge.*

It is obvious that nothing good will come out if you assign a project to a data scientist who simply lacks skills and/or experience to tackle it. Throwing someone in at the deep end is not an effective teaching technique in data science, where even the most basic skills is not something we are born with.

It may be less obvious that a never-ending stream of tasks that are too *easy* also constitutes a problem.

As we discussed in Chapter 6, a data scientist should strive to automate away repetitive tasks, but not all easy tasks are repetitive. For example, if a data scientist is often getting "ad hoc" requests that are rarely the same, it may be practically impossible to try and get rid of them for good by developing self-serving reports. A viable solution might be to redirect such requests to a junior data scientist or intern, who would find them both more challenging and more conducive to their professional growth.

This is another reason why it is beneficial for organizations to have data scientists not only with diverse backgrounds and skill sets, but also of different levels of experience.

> It is beneficial for organizations to have data scientists not only with diverse backgrounds and skill sets, but also of different levels of experience.

achievement

A well-defined goal with a clear purpose and a level of challenge adequate to the data scientist's ability is a great start. Achieving this goal requires getting another set of things right:

- data,
- autonomy,
- focus,
- time,
- culture.

Data

An organization where data scientists are perfectly happy with the data they have got access to is an exception, not the rule. The rule is that most organizations suffer from a combination of the following:

- Not all potentially useful data is collected and stored.
- Data scientists have limited access to the data.
- Data is poorly organized and documented.

This often happens due to company leadership assuming that data science only requires data scientists. Or *a* data scientist. The latter then has to wear multiple hats: data engineer, data scientist, business analyst, product owner... This does not necessarily mean they will not deliver valuable insights, but they will definitely be less efficient than they would be in a team of people, each an expert in their domain.

Autonomy

Micromanagement—management style whereby a manager closely controls the work of their subordinates—is a problem in many a workplace. In data science, it is often exacerbated by the manager's poor grasp of data science best practices.

I was reviewing a report by a data scientist from another office when I noticed a missing zero baseline on a bar chart:

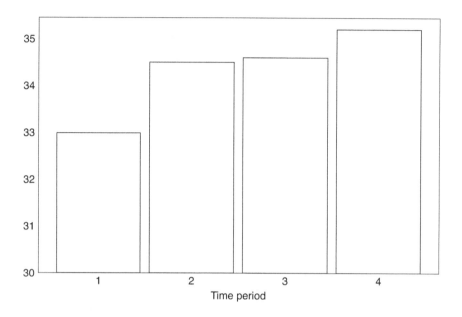

This looks like a nice bar chart that shows a clear positive trend. But a closer look reveals that the bars start at 30, not zero. Changing the baseline to zero would give the chart a much less exciting look:

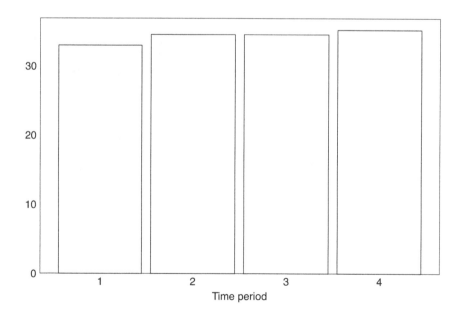

This could be an honest mistake or an attempt to exaggerate a trend in the data in support of someone's pet theory. I got in touch with the data scientist behind the report and pointed it out that manipulating the baseline like that could be misleading. "I know," was his response, "but the business manager told me to do it."

At the other extreme lies a complete lack of direction and supervision. It is not uncommon for a data science team to "break away" from the rest of the organization, with data scientists keeping themselves busy with side projects and Kaggle competitions.

At the highest level of abstraction, the ideal leadership style boils down to a simple recipe:

- hire good people,
- show them a problem that needs to be solved,
- leave them alone.

Thus, the expectation of a data scientist should be not to complete assigned work, but to solve business problems. For a bigger data science team, a good practice is so-called matrix management, when a data scientist reports to the team lead (who is in charge of *what* needs to be done) as

> The expectation of a data scientist should be not to complete assigned work, but to solve business problems.

well as a "tech" lead (who advises as to *how* it should be done), the latter typically being one of the senior data scientists. This way, the team lead is less tempted to micromanage, whereas the tech lead is unlikely to want to micromanage in the first place—he or she is already busy helping people who *ask* for help.

Focus

Distraction is a major issue in jobs that involve solving complex problems.

Software developers and data scientists belong to the category of "concentrators" using the four employee types identified by Microsoft's Workplace Advantage program, other categories being "travelers," "orchestrators" and "providers."

Solving a complex problem requires holding and manipulating information in your working memory. This takes concentration. You are building a house of cards. The more complex the problem, the more stories you have to painstakingly put on top of each other.

Any interruption—a team-mate asking you a question, a notification on your phone, even a conversation taking place nearby—can yank you out of your thought process, so that you will have to start from the beginning when the interruption is over. The interruption is a puppy that runs into your study and brings your house of cards down. When you need to concentrate on a difficult problem, you want the door to your study shut, to keep the puppies away.

This metaphor can be taken literally when you have the luxury of working from home. Having a focused time can actually be a matter of simply closing the door. This does not work when you

> Focused time becomes a scarce resource you have got to fight for.

have to share your workplace with others. Focused time becomes a scarce resource you have got to fight for.

Open offices became popular in the 1990s, with cubicles going out of fashion. They are supposed to facilitate interactions, but it is not clear if they do. One study found that when companies switched to open offices, face-to-face interactions fell by 70% (Bernstein and Waber, 2019).

Another problem is that not all interactions are desirable. In open space, there is no such thing as a conversation between *two* people. When two people want to talk, most of the time they do not go off to a quiet space somewhere. They end up interrupting others' concentration. This may sometimes help keep everyone "in the loop," but the loss of concentration and productivity is not worth it. Unsurprisingly, data scientists working in open space often block out the outside world using noise-cancelling headphones.

Over the course of my career as data scientist, I have worked in various environments:

- open space,
- room with non-data people,
- room with other data scientists,
- on my own (either in office or at home).

I can confirm that working in open space or sharing room with people from other departments is detrimental to data scientist's productivity. Sharing room with other data scientists is more acceptable, as there is more of useful interactions and fewer of those I would rather not have. Of course, nothing beats working on your own. That is, until you need someone's help.

Carl Howe writes in his blog post "Equipping Your Data Science Team to Work from Home"[1]: "Like tigers and koala bears, we data scientists are fairly solitary creatures. We typically eschew meetings, embrace focus time, and block out distractions to focus on our work. And on those rare times when we need help, our typical reaction is to walk over to a colleague's desk and brainstorm an answer."

Another scourge of focus is meetings.

The post titled "Meetings are Toxic" on Basecamp's blog "Signal v. Noise"[2] sums it up well: "Meetings are one of the worst kinds of workplace interruptions. They're held too frequently, run too long, and involve more people than necessary."

There is a special kind of meetings. They are usually daily and take place in the morning. More often than not the team gathers in front of a board with sticky notes or something similar used to track team's projects. "Morning stand-up."

As far as I can tell, morning stand-ups serve two purposes:

- The manager can conveniently keep tabs on everyone without having to talk to each team member individually.

- People who like to talk have a great opportunity to do exactly that. And people around them have to listen, as it is extremely difficult to come up with a good excuse and walk away. You can get a phone call about a family emergency only so many times before it gets suspicious.

It is the same problem as with the open space: someone is having a conversation and everyone around has to listen in. Only this time you cannot even save yourself with noise-cancelling headphones. At least not without coming across as passive-aggressive.

I used to hate morning stand-ups. The only reason I do not now is that I am not having them anymore.

> I used to hate morning stand-ups. The only reason I do not now is that I am not having them anymore.

First of all, they would interrupt my morning flow. I would usually arrive at the office about half an hour before the stand-up. It would make little sense to spend 15–20 minutes getting into the "zone" only to be abruptly jerked out of it right away. Eventually, I gave up on the idea of working before the meeting and started coming in half an hour later. Win-win.

Second, I would not be interested in listening about what other data scientists did yesterday and were going to do today. It might be useful for the team to have a rough idea of what everyone is getting up to, e.g., to avoid double-work, but simply sending out a short email when taking on a new project would suffice. And if someone needed help with their project, they would not have waited until next morning to ask for it.

When it was my turn to fill the silence, I would try and get away with a one-sentence description of my project, or even simply point at the corresponding sticky note on the board—"yes, still working on that." I never saw why anyone would need to know the details if they were not part of the project. When the project was finished, I would send out an email with a carefully crafted summary, which others would be able to read at their convenience. And even if someone had reasons to be curious, they were welcome to catch me in the kitchen area, and I would happily answer their questions—no need to hurt innocent by-standers.

Meetings eat into another valuable resource:

Time

It takes time, often more than outsiders would have expected, to understand the problem, gather and clean data, run the analysis, or train a model, and deliver useable results. Companies, especially those that have only started investing in data science, may want immediate results. A data scientist who finds themselves in such situation can only try and focus on two things:

- deliver *something* as quickly as possible, to show return on investment in data science as well as boost its credibility;
- delicately point out what stands between the company and data-driven riches: usually lack of data and...

Culture

Some problems can be solved by throwing money at them. Creating a "data culture" is not one of those.

Unless a business is data-driven by its nature (e.g., ML/AI startup) or has been founded by data-savvy geeks, people who run it are making decisions based on their opinions and intuition "by default." This is how they have always been doing it. A decision to invest in data analytics is not going to change that. Nor hiring a few data engineers and data scientists.

What creates a data culture is the virtuous cycle of using data to improve business processes and their outcomes, which boosts the credibility of and investment in data and analytics. The more open the company and its leadership to novel practices, the faster data culture will proliferate.

As a simple rule, there has to be at least one person whose job description includes "data evangelism." And that person has be good at selling a vision.

reward

This is the last component of goal-achievement-reward cycle and the easiest to overlook. It is easy to overlook from an outsider's perspective. If someone is regularly achieving their work goals, it takes perception and empathy to ask them, "Do you find your work rewarding enough?"

It is not that difficult to overlook a lack of reward even from the insider's perspective. Goal-oriented people with high conscientiousness may "skip" the reward part altogether. They will complete project after project until the lack of reward catches up with them in the shape of burnout or, at the very least, sudden onset of job dissatisfaction.

The novelty of starting out in a new field or at a new company, as well as intellectually challenging problems, may serve as an implicit reward that will keep a data scientist going for a while. In the long run, however, it is vital that the following components are present: impact, fair recognition, and growth.

Impact

If "unclear goals" was the second biggest source of data scientists' frustration according to my little survey, lack of impact on the business was the biggest, with nearly 50% of respondents picking it out of a multitude of options.

A typical data scientist is already in a position where their impact on the overall success of the organization is not immediately obvious. In Chapter 1, we looked at "data impact pathway" examples of a mobile gaming company and a football club. In both examples, the data scientist was five steps away from the core business value.

In November 2014, King launched the long-awaited sequel to their flagship game *Candy Crush*—*Candy Crush Soda*, with big-time promotional events in New York and London. It was a make-or-break release for the company, as many doubted if it would be anywhere close to the success of the original game. As it turned out, it was close. *Candy Crush Soda* immediately became the second-most grossing game by King, and I remember at least 1 day when its revenue surpassed that of the original *Candy Crush*.

I had the privilege of being the data scientist "embedded" in the development team, working closely with a producer and two level designers. Our main priority was to optimize the first few dozen levels of the game. We had several months to figure out the best way to get the players "hooked" by giving them the most fun to play levels with the right level of challenge, as well as introducing and explaining new game mechanics at the right time.

A beta version of the game was "soft launched" (released under a fake name) in a few select countries, so we were able to run several A/B tests and test our hypotheses as to what worked better. For example, we discovered that measuring retention rate after 7 days was not enough. Subjecting players to a harder level sequence could result in a lower retention after 1 week compared to an easier sequence, but higher—after 2 weeks. (We theorized that harder levels had a higher appeal for those players who were more likely to stick around for a while.)

Having picked the "winner" level sequence, we ran another A/B test to compare its performance to that of the very first sequence, which would have been used if we had not run any tests at all. It showed that we had improved retention rate by several percentage points, which is a big deal for a mobile free-to-play game.

So, the game was a clear success and had a big impact on the success of the business as a whole—everyone in the development team could give themselves a pat on the back. Optimization of the early levels was a success and had a big impact on the success of the game—the producer and level designers had every right to be pleased with themselves. But what was my impact as data scientist? Of course, *someone* had to crunch the numbers, but did I do a better or worse job than another data scientist would have done?

> Even when everyone around is celebrating the success of a project, it is easy for a data scientist to quietly doubt the significance of their contribution.

> Even when everyone around is celebrating the success of a project, it is easy for a data scientist to quietly doubt the significance of their contribution.

The problem of a long impact pathway is often exacerbated by a lack of feedback loop, where data scientist delivers a product (analysis, report, data-driven tool) and hears little to nothing from the end-users.

This lack of feedback loop was present to some extent in all organizations I have been at. Sometimes I would be genuinely surprised that people were using something I had made a while ago and, having not heard back, believed to have been a failed project.

This can be mitigated by generally improving communication between the data science team and its stakeholders, which is never a bad idea. However, to get *consistently* strong feedback, some kind of follow-up on a completed project needs to be part of the process. And whoever is running the data science team is likely to be in the best position to make that happen.

Nothing should be delivered into the "void." You created a customer lifetime value prediction model for the marketing department—are they actually using it to optimize their advertising spend? You built a product performance dashboard—who is looking at it and how often? You analyzed an A/B test—has the best-performing option been implemented? Someone asked you to "pull some data"—did they read your email, and did it help them?

If you do this for *every* project you deliver, not only will you have a chance to feel that you are making an impact, but you will also understand what has value and what does not. This will let you have a say in the planning and prioritizing of data science projects—one of the things that separate a senior data scientist from a junior one.

> Have a say in the planning and prioritizing of data science projects — one of the things that separate a senior data scientist from a junior one.

Fair Recognition

We all want recognition for our effort and contribution. Recognition usually comes in the form of positive feedback, salary raises and promotions. What makes it more complicated is that we also want to be recognized *fairly*.

Even monkeys, who are generally accepted to be not as intelligent as people, are sensitive to unfairness. They can be perfectly happy to perform a simple task for a piece of cucumber but will reject it if they have seen another monkey get a grape (a tastier treat) for the same task (Brosnan and de Waal 2003). This shows that the need for fairness is part of our biological make-up.

Data science is a new, still rapidly developing discipline. The data science team is often a new, fast-growing part of the company. What can happen, particularly if the company itself is growing, is a paradoxical situation, when a newly hired data scientist negotiates a starting salary that is higher than that of someone who joined the company a year or 2 earlier.

Most companies frown upon employees disclosing their salaries. But people talk. Another paradox ensues: a more senior data scientist knows that they are paid less than their junior colleagues, but they are not supposed to know that and cannot openly challenge the status quo. This creates an incentive for the more experienced, yet underpaid, employees to look for a move to another company, where they can potentially negotiate a 10%–20% increase in the same position.

It is not uncommon for the company to offer a substantial raise to an employee who has got an offer from another company. Yet even if the employee accepts this offer and stays, there is bound to be a bad aftertaste on both sides. The company knows that the employee has been looking for greener pastures and will have less confidence in a long-term future together. The employee will feel that they have had to bend the company's arm into fairly recognizing their contribution.

"We have no problem giving a raise to those who deserve it. All they need to do is ask" may look like a sensible position for an employer. But not every employee feels comfortable walking into their manager's office and declaring they want more. Many, at the very least, will want to have a job offer from another company to back up their claim and have a "plan B" in case things go south. This makes for a different conversation, with no feeling of a good will.

All this unpleasantness could be prevented if the company, or the data science manager in particular, looked out for discrepancies between employees' contribution and compensation. As a manager, you should never underestimate people's sensitivity to unfair treatment.

> As a manager, you should never underestimate people's sensitivity to unfair treatment.

Growth

Career advancement is one of the top two motivations for data science and analytics professionals, along with salary (2018 survey by

Butch Works[3]). If a company wants to retain its best data scientists, it needs to offer them growth opportunities, which is easier said than done.

There are three directions along which a data scientist can "grow":

- vertical, e.g., data scientist → team manager → chief data officer;
- lateral, e.g., data scientist → product manager;
- depth, e.g., data scientist → senior data scientist → principal data scientist.

Vertical growth requires people and project management skills. Already after the first promotion, data science skills per se become relatively unimportant.

A lateral move puts a similar emphasis on the skills required by the new domain (typically, business or product management), with data science skills having only some carry-over.

Going "deep" is the only direction that requires further development of data science skills, but even then they are not the ultimate measure of seniority. Describing what technical skills someone needs to master to progress to the next level does not take into account how well they *apply* these skills.

A thoughtful and result-oriented analyst with solid Excel skills and understanding of what makes the business tick can deliver more value than a scatter-brain data scientist whose greatest desire is to use the latest tool they read about in their next project. The latter may be proficient with advanced data science tools, but would you rank them above the former?

Demanding that a data scientist be handy with a specific tool may push them towards using that tool regardless of whether it is appropriate. You may end up replacing the goal of solving business problems with the goal of getting experience using various tools. Not good.

* * *

We are going to talk about different types of data scientists and what directions they may be interested in further on, but in the ideal world these three directions should be equally viable. In the real world, they are usually not.

Towards the end of my time at King, around 2017–2018, there had been established a sensible career path for a data scientist (DS): junior DS → DS → senior DS → principal DS, with corresponding salary brackets.

There was also available a lateral move into business performance management, with its own, very similar career track: junior business performance manager (BPM) → BPM → senior BPM.

For a reason that I was unable to establish, the powers that be decided on the following career "fork":

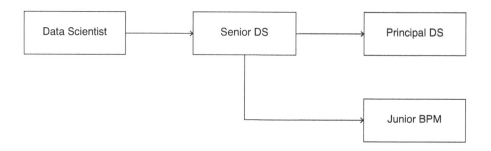

That is, as a senior data scientist, which usually implied 3+ years of experience, you could choose between supposedly equal aspirations of working your way towards the role of principal DS, the final step of the "depth" career path, or becoming a junior BPM, a role often given to a recent graduate with a non-STEM degree.

Not only did that make little sense, it also implicitly undermined the role of data science in the otherwise very data-mature company.

data scientist types

While all data scientists have something in common, they *are* quite different from each other. Outsiders tend to overlook in-group differences. For example, people who grew up in an ethnically homogenous environment famously struggle when they travel to a place populated by people of a different race—everyone looks so similar. Same with data scientists: to a less discerning outsider they may all look like geeks only interested in statistics and programming, whereas reality—as always—is rather more nuanced.

When people talk about different varieties of data scientists, they usually classify them based on their background and skills. For example, "The Care and Feeding of Data Scientists" (D'Agostino and Malone 2019) talks about three archetypes based on background:

- PhD graduate in a quantitative field,
- graduate of a data science master's program or data science bootcamp,
- software engineer turned data scientist.

This is a useful classification and knowing data scientist's background makes it easier to identify their strengths and weaknesses. However, while data scientists' background and skills are common discussion topics, their inner drives are less so. When hiring and managing data scientists it is important to be able to recognize different types based on their primary needs and interests. The following classification addresses it.

* * *

Most endeavors of human progress can be imagined as a sequence of five distinct steps:

1. **Idea**: we identify a problem or opportunity (two sides of the coin, really).
2. **Theory**: we understand how things work.
3. **Tools**: we develop and master technology.
4. **Solution**: we combine theory and technology to solve the problem.
5. **Recognition**: we ascend in a competence-based social hierarchy.

In a professional environment, most people are primarily focused on one or two of the above, and data scientists are no exception. While a data scientist's focus can shift over the course of their professional life, at any given point they can be roughly classified using archetypes corresponding to each step.

Idea: "Entrepreneur"

Extroverted and sociable, likes talking to people and discussing ideas. Usually has a few good ideas of their own but may lack the discipline and patience for thorough research and implementation.

In all honesty, being a data scientist is not for them, and rather sooner than later they will either move to a different position or a different company. If they are worth their money, it is best to find a position that suits their strengths, e.g., as a manager/owner of a product with a high degree of innovation.

Theory: "Academic"

Comfortable with statistics and mathematics in general, likes to ponder over complicated problems, not necessarily arriving at a practical solution.

They can make a great *research* data scientist but should be supported by business- and tech-savvy people to make sure that research eventually translates into business value.

Usually unambitious career-wise, they are happy to stay put as long as they are surrounded by nice people and have the opportunity to work on intellectually challenging problems.

Tools: "Geek"

Above all wants to play with the latest technology. If into machine learning, is likely to be a Kaggle grandmaster.[4]

They are very efficient when a data science project requires using a new shiny tool, and a complete opposite when it does not. Their best chance to shine is when they *enable* other data scientists in larger organizations by helping them expand their toolbox. Form a data science *technology* team, and they can be your most impactful employees.

Geeks are highly susceptible to FOMO (fear of missing out). When it happens, you may hear them complain:

- We don't have big data, we just have a bunch of spreadsheets/ SQL database, while everyone else is using Hadoop/Hive/Spark.
- We're not doing any machine learning/deep learning/ reinforcement learning projects.
- We're not using <whatever the next big thing is>.

Solution: "Doer"

Conscientious and result-oriented, focuses on getting things done and cares little about how. Likes clearly defined goals and autonomy in reaching them. Prefers working alone or with a small number of like-minded people.

They are the staple of business and product data science, but may struggle with research and technology, when they lack the feeling of immediate purpose. They can make a good mentor but will probably struggle as a people manager.

Primarily motivated by being useful and appreciated.

Recognition: "Careerist"

Confident and always looking for a way up. Capable of doing good work as long as it increases their chances to get noticed and promoted. If it does not happen for them in this company, they will probably start looking elsewhere as soon as their CV allows.

Requires a clear career path.

* * *

As with most people classifications, any given data scientist may manifest features of more than one archetype. As employer, you may be looking for particular combinations based on your situation and needs:

- a company that would like to become more data-driven—Entrepreneur/Doer;
- technology company that would like to grow their analytics team—Geek/Careerist;
- AI startup—a bit of everything.

When building a data science team, you want to make sure you are covering all the archetypes (in a small team, perhaps with the exception of Careerist, as it is probably covered by you, since you are building a data science team). Knowing what kind of archetype you are lacking, you can hire smarter.

Data Scientist Types

	Drive	Strengths	Weaknesses	Ideal Position
Entrepreneur *Idea*	Find new opportunities	Outgoing and full of ideas.	May lack discipline and patience to see ideas through.	Data-savvy business or product manager in a growing or evolving business.
Academic *Theory*	Solve complicated theoretical problems	Comfortable with math and can research a problem deeply.	May focus on the wrong problem and/or fail to develop a practical solution.	Research data scientist supported by business- and tech-savvy people.
Geek *Tools*	Play with new technology	Quick to grasp and use new tools.	May focus on how instead of what or why. Susceptible to FOMO.	Engineering data scientist or part of data science technology team.
Doer *Solution*	Be useful	Conscientious and gets things done.	May focus on the work and forget about people and bigger picture.	Business or product data scientist with clearly defined goals.
Careerist *Recognition*	Rise up the corporate ladder	Confident and driven.	May focus on how they are perceived, not necessarily what they actually do.	One level above where they were a year ago, in a fast-growing business.

glossary

Kaggle.com is an online platform that hosts machine learning competitions.

works cited

"Monkeys Reject Unequal Pay" / S. Brosnan, and F. de Waal / 2003 *Nature* 425: 297–299.

"The Truth about Open Offices" / E. Bernstein, and B. Waber / *Harvard Business Review* (November–December 2019).

The Care and Feeding of Data Scientists / Michelangelo D'Agostino, and Katie Malone / 2019 O'Reilly Media.

notes

1 https://blog.rstudio.com/2020/05/12/equipping-wfh-data-science-teams/.

2 https://m.signalvnoise.com/meetings-are-toxic/.

3 https://www.burtchworks.com/2018/06/18/survey-results-what-motivates-analytics-pros-data-scientists-to-change-jobs/.

4 https://www.kaggle.com/progression.

measuring performance

The previous chapter focused on what data scientists need to be happy and productive. Measuring employee satisfaction is outside the scope of this book,[1] but a chapter on how to measure productivity will make for a fitting conclusion.

Measuring things is a big part of data science. Making up KPI's and tracking them is the foundation of business intelligence. It would be reasonable to expect that one of the things a data scientist can help to measure is their own performance. In practice, putting a number on the value of their work can be challenging.

In my 8 years in data science, I only once was in a meeting whose main point was to discuss how data scientists' performance ought to be evaluated. The whole data science team was present, and an HR person was facilitating. It was an hour-long discussion, with a lot of issues raised and a lot of good points made.

The outcome of the meeting?—We solved it! Only joking. Not only did we not "solve" the problem of measuring performance, we did not even come up with any improvements to the existing process.

We are going to take a close look at several approaches to evaluating a data scientist's performance. To make it easier to keep track of them and relate them to each other, we will place them on a spectrum: something as objective and easily measurable as *time at work* on the left, and someone's subjective *opinion* on the right.

Time	Throughput	Goals	Opinion

DOI: 10.1201/9781003057420-12

time

Time spent at work is the most straightforward measure. You come in at 9 am, leave at 9 pm = 8 working hours (minus lunch break). It is a viable performance indicator for jobs with a fixed (or stable enough) value production rate. The kind of job where being present equals working. On the streets of Japan, you can sometimes see a person standing still and holding a roadworks sign. The hours they put in accurately reflect their performance.

A job that involves solving challenging problems makes time spent *at work* and time spent *working* two separate concepts. The widely accepted mindset is that a respectable workday is 8 hours. Yet, typically, less than half of it is spent on one's primary duties. (Personally, I

> A job that involves solving challenging problems makes time spent *at work* and time spent *working* two separate concepts.

consider any day when I have had 3 hours of focused work as fairly productive.) The rest is filled with socializing, personal admin, browsing the Internet—anything to pad out the actual work. There are very few organizations that can openly accept that the actual workday can be done by noon.

Blind, a discussion community for professionals, conducted a survey[2] of 2,601 remote workers in January of 2021.

Forty two percent of the respondents reported to work 4 hours a day or less.

To me, this is not at all surprising. Take away coffee breaks and watercooler chat—and this is close to what you would get at the office, too.

Furthermore, when it comes to thinking, people are sometimes more productive outside of work. A moment of ingenuity in the shower may be worth a whole day of being interrupted in the office. There is no way to measure time spent on work-related thinking. Until we have perfected brain scanning technology, that is. For the moment, paying attention to how much time people spend at work does nothing but undermines the importance of working smart. If the focus is on showing up, people will show up. Some will *just* show up. They will be happy with this system, but they will not be your most productive or most impactful employees. Those who want to be productive and to make an impact will go looking for an environment where it is appreciated.

If you are a data scientist and you are being judged by how many hours you spend at the office (or online, if you are working from home), you are probably at the wrong place.

It is interesting to note the influence of culture on the attitude towards time at work.

Japanese culture is famous for its emphasis on teamwork and putting the (perceived) effort in: it is unimaginable for a typical office worker to leave at 5 pm sharp, unless they have got a good excuse, e.g., doctor's appointment. The norm is to stay for an extra hour or two, regardless of whether or not there is urgent work to be done.

Swedish attitude in this respect could not be more different. Leaving at 3 pm to pick up kids from the daycare raises no questions. I remember a corporate memo that gently reminded everyone not to make jokes about colleagues leaving early because that might hurt their feelings. (I am not making this up.)

throughput

In the context of a data science team, throughput would normally mean the number of tasks finished in a period of time (typically, a month or a quarter). In terms of measuring performance, it is a big step up from time. If a data scientist takes long lunch breaks but has the same throughput as the rest of the team, they are clearly *doing* as much even though they are *working* less.

Measuring throughput makes sense when quantity is the only thing that matters. Since it is safe to assume that quality always matters in data science, throughput is a viable metric only in situations when quality does not vary much. For example, a centralized team of data analysts handling ad-hoc requests from business users may find that they do not need anything more sophisticated than counting the number of requests handled by each analyst.

If requests are simple enough, e.g., pulling and processing data, the implicit quality control by the end-users, who will notice if the numbers do not make sense, may be just enough to ensure that the quality of the analysts' work does not fall below a certain level.

If requests are small enough, the difference in their difficulty will average out over time. So, if an analyst consistently handles more requests, it is likely that they *are* objectively more productive.

Measuring throughput is unlikely to work well in a different situation. A few examples:

- A standalone analyst "embedded" in a product team. Even if they are handling a steady stream of ad-hoc requests, there is no frame of reference except their past performance. Even if there is another analyst, embedded in a different team, their performance may not be directly comparable. The proverbial apples to oranges.

- Anything where quantity is overshadowed by the difficulty of the task or the importance of quality. Writing programming code is a good example. As Bill Gates said, "Measuring programming progress by lines of code is like measuring aircraft building progress by weight."

- A team of specialized data scientists working on projects of different nature. If one data scientist is researching machine learning algorithms while another is building a dashboard, it is impossible to compare their performance using a single metric.

One has to be careful when trying to quantify people's work. A metric may make sense in theory yet get subverted in practice. What is commonly known as Goodhart's law states, "When a measure becomes a target, it ceases to be a good measure" (Strathern, 1997)

When I worked in customer support of a software company, we would use the number of resolved cases as the main KPI, which was tied to a bonus system. Some team members would take "quantity over quality" to the extreme. They would barely read what the customer had written, send them a canned response and mark the case as resolved. Most of the time this would have failed to solve the customer's problem. Some customers would write again, some would give up. Either way, this approach worked well to boost the daily number of "resolved" cases into three-digit numbers.

In the end, we had to introduce a quality control system, so that both quantity and quality mattered. It did not solve the problem completely, but it made it harder to get away with sloppy work.

goal achievement

Any scenario more complex than a team of data analysts handling a steady influx of bite-size tasks demands an approach more flexible than a single metric. A popular choice is to set individual goals for each data scientist and quantify their achievement. A data scientist can have a set of goals of different nature:

- **Operational**: support a team or multiple teams on an ongoing basis. Goals of this kind are difficult to quantify unless it is the "throughput" scenario. Feedback from the supported team(s) may be the only thing to go by. This is not necessarily a bad situation. A simple question, "On a scale of 1–5, how satisfied are you with the data support you have received in the last 3 months?" asked to the respective team managers over a few periods and/or about several different data scientists will provide useful data with little overhead.

- **Business project**: for example, help launch a new product. It may be tempting to use business KPI's to quantify the data scientist's performance. Success of a product presents enticingly measurable objectives, such as number of users, retention and conversion rates, revenue etc. Yet it is important to differentiate between input and output. We control the input. This is where the performance ought to be measured. We do not control the output, which may depend on any number of external factors.

  Success of the product is the output, which depends on the product quality, competition and much else. Data scientist's work, which, in this case, is the input, affects the output only to *some* extent—via the product quality, and even that depends on the buy-in from the product team.

  Whoever wants to measure the data scientist's performance will do well to isolate the input from the output. If the only option is to get feedback from the product team, then it is best to do it *before* the product is launched, before its success or failure has affected everyone's perception.

- **Data science project**: for example, build an interactive KPI report. This scenario is similar to business project, only now the data scientist themselves is the product team, and whatever they are building—the product. The product KPI's—its popularity and perceived value—become much more indicative of how well the data scientist has done.

Setting measurable goals can provide an adequate framework for an objective evaluation of data scientists' performance. Regardless of the nature of the goals, their achievement can be expressed as a percentage, and the overall performance can be calculated as a weighted sum.

Here is an example of a quarterly evaluation:

Goal	Achievement	Weight	Weighted Value (%)
Support marketing team	80% (grade 4 out 5)	0.2	16
Support new product launch	90% (4.5/5)	0.5	45
Build product KPI dashboard	100% (everyone loves it)	0.3	30
Total			91

Even without any context whatsoever (past evaluations or other data scientists), this is a useful set of numbers. A quick glance is enough to understand that the data scientist has performed well enough, with some room for improvement.

Assigning each goal a weight allows to differentiate goals by difficulty and/or importance. You may require that the weights add up to exactly 1, then the total value will always fall between 0% and 100%, which makes it easy to interpret. This works well for a standalone data scientist. If you need to compare the performance of multiple data scientists, you may do better without the limitation on goal weights. If a particularly productive team member takes on twice as much workload as you would expect from the average data scientist and deals with it perfectly, then it is only fair to score him or her at 200%.

Goal achievement framework provides the flexibility and versatility missing in the throughput approach. It is applicable to practically any setup, be it a centralized or distributed data science team, a standalone data scientist or a group, a large number of similar tasks or a handful of highly specialized long-term projects. However, the framework also presents new challenges:

- The goals may not be known in advance. In data science, one often learns as they go, not before they go. New goals are often born, unexpectedly, in response to business challenges, discovery of new possibilities, or ideas generated within the data science team itself.

If goals are set as part of an annual or biannual performance review, they are unlikely all to survive until the next review. The data scientist and their line manager may have to review the goals on a more frequent basis (e.g., monthly) to keep them up to date.

- Goal weights and achievement rates require subjective judgment. A good practice is to set these values in collaboration between the data scientist and their line manager. If the two do not always see eye to eye, it can put additional strain on the relationship.

This may be further exacerbated by managerial changes. In my 4 years at King, only once did I have two consecutive performance reviews with the same team manager. Otherwise, I would set goals with one manager and have to review them with another. Reaching an agreement between two people is challenging enough. When one of these people is replaced half a year later, keeping the agreement to everyone's satisfaction takes a small miracle.

---

opinion

This is a popular choice "by default." With no explicit performance evaluation framework, the only input into decision-making for raises/promotions/etc. is the subjective opinion of one or several people—line manager, tech lead, the manager of the team the data scientist is embedded into, and so on.

The obvious shortcoming of relying on people's opinions is that the latter are easily influenced by factors external to the data scientist's work:

- **Overall success of the relevant teams/products**: Similar to using business KPI's in the goal achievement framework, taking into account the overall success of the team and/or product the data scientist has been working with would contaminate input (what we should measure) with output (what we are tempted to measure). It takes a great deal of cognitive discipline not to do it subconsciously.

- **Personal relationships**: Even less relevant than the overall success. Even harder to ignore. It is important to make a distinction between *working* relationships, which *are* an important part of data scientist's job, and *personal* relationships, which may be a bonus, but should not be reflected in their performance evaluation.

A data scientist needs to be able to communicate "the bitter truth" without any concerns for how it may affect their image. He or she needs to be able to disagree with people regardless of their rank. He or she needs to be able to go against the popular opinion. It may be precisely their job to try and change other people's opinion.

If a data scientist's performance is evaluated based on someone's opinion, it is crucial that this person can separate their opinion of the data scientist's work from their opinion of the data scientist as a person. And this is an unattainable ideal.

> If a data scientist's performance is evaluated based on someone's opinion, it is crucial that this person can separate their opinion of the data scientist's work from their opinion of the data scientist as a person.

- **Perception**: A good example is mistaking confidence for competence. Real-life data does not always yield itself to neat patterns, clear trends or statistical significance. An honest data scientist often has to say, "I don't know." They can be perceived as being indecisive, meek, wishy-washy. A less scrupulous data scientist, who is more comfortable jumping to conclusions and sweeping inconvenient details under the rug, and who makes positive statements in a loud voice will often be perceived as simply a better data scientist.

> An honest data scientist often has to say, "I don't know."

All of the above can be mitigated to some extent by aggregating subjective opinions of several people, especially if they come from different branches of the organization's hierarchy. If you combine opinions of the line manager, tech lead, product owner, the junior colleague the data scientist has been mentoring, the resulting average (weighted, if necessary) has a good chance to accurately reflect the data scientist's true performance.

The opinion framework may work well for a distributed and diverse data science team operating in a fast-changing environment. When setting, weighting, and tracking goals creates too much overhead, a simple survey of 4–5 people a data scientist has worked with in the last 3 months can be just the thing.

The opinion framework will always depend on the culture of truth and meritocracy, but if it is not there no performance evaluation framework will compensate for it.

* * *

This chapter provided but a brief overview of several approaches to measuring the performance of a data scientist. It is absolutely possible, and often beneficial, to use their variations and combinations. It is not much of a stretch of imagination to come up with a plausible example of a senior data scientist who is evaluated based on all four approaches:

- **Time**: spent in mentoring sessions with junior colleagues. The company is always hiring, and the data scientist is expected to make herself available for face-to-face sessions with new starters on a regular basis. It is practically impossible to measure the "quality" of a session, which also depends on the mentee, so this is a rare case when showing up equals working.

- **Throughput**: number of conference talks. The company wants exposure and expects every senior data scientist to speak at 3–5 conferences a year. The quality of a talk is controlled by the sheer desire not to embarrass oneself in front of audience, so a simple count of talks given is enough.

- **Opinion**: that of the lead of a long-term cross-team project in which the data scientist takes part.

All of the above are treated as goals, with the end-of-year evaluation looking like this:

Goal	Achievement	Weight	Weighted value (%)
Mentorship 200 hours/year	120% (~240 hours logged)	0.2	24
Conference talks 4 talks/year	75% (only 3 this year)	0.3	22.5
Project X	80% (4/5 from the project lead)	0.5	40
Total			86.5

As with many things in data science, the optimal solution depends on the particular situation. Very much so when it comes to managing and evaluating a data science team. And you always have a better shot at finding a solution that works for you when you know what have been tried by others. "A smart person learns from their mistakes, a wise person—from the mistakes of others."

works cited

"'Improving Ratings': Audit in the British University System" / M. Strathern / 1997 *European Review*, 305—321.

notes

1 There are whole books on the topic, e.g., *Measuring Employee Satisfaction* (2008) by Ingrid Goovaerts, Barry.Whittaker, Joanne Lawrence, Heidi Lampi.

2 https://www.teamblind.com/blog/index.php/2021/01/21/are-remote-workers-actually-working/.

index

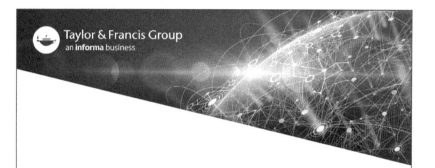